The Lost Leaders

The Lost Leaders

How Corporate America Loses Women Leaders

Rebekah S. Heppner

First published in 2013 by
PALGRAVE MACMILLAN®
in the United States—a division of St. Martin's Press LLC,
175 Fifth Avenue, New York, NY 10010.

Where this book is distributed in the UK, Europe and the rest of the world,
this is by Palgrave Macmillan, a division of Macmillan Publishers Limited,
registered in England, company number 785998, of Houndmills,
Basingstoke, Hampshire RG21 6XS.

Palgrave Macmillan is the global academic imprint of the above companies
and has companies and representatives throughout the world.

Palgrave® and Macmillan® are registered trademarks in the United States,
the United Kingdom, Europe and other countries.

ISBN: 978-1-137-35612-3

Library of Congress Cataloging-in-Publication Data

Heppner, Rebekah S., 1954–
    The lost leaders : how corporate America loses women leaders / by
    Rebekah S. Heppner.
        pages cm
    Includes bibliographical references.
    ISBN 978-1-137-35612-3 (alk. paper)
        1. Women executives—United States—Biography.
    2. Businesswomen—United States—Biography. 3. Sex discrimination
    against women—United States. 4. Corporate culture—United States.
    I. Title.

HD6054.4.U6H47 2013
331.4'81658400922—dc23   2013019168

A catalogue record of the book is available from the British Library.

Design by Newgen Knowledge Works (P) Ltd., Chennai, India.

First edition: September 2013

10 9 8 7 6 5 4 3 2 1

To all the women who tried to build careers in Corporate America,
those who are still trying,
and those who will try, and succeed, in the future.

CONTENTS

ACKNOWLEDGMENTS

First, I extend my deep appreciation to the formers executives who shared their stories with me so willingly. Their enthusiasm for my research gives me hope for the future for women, both in the workplace and in society; they have remained hopeful and optimistic despite the obstacles they encountered in their careers.

I also want to thank the early readers of my manuscript. Andrea Spears and Joanie Halfaker read parts of an early version of this work and provided their usual candid advice. Katie Dumala and Kim Hanna dutifully read two complete versions and provided specific recommendations on how to make it better each time. Ivette Kaptzan and Linda Wright read the second version and provided valuable feedback from the current workplace.

Many thanks go to my writing accountability partner, Kathy McDonald, who asked me to help keep her on track and ended up helping me so much more. I look forward to sharing many future writing projects, and cups of coffee, with her.

Last, I thank my eldest sister, Connie Heppner, who read an early version of the book, but who also shared her knowledge of the book business and who has provided personal advice and support that have helped me in so many ways over the years.

Introduction

Business leaders are being lost—in a business world that so desperately needs leadership today. Although women now represent half of all managers, they still hold less than 10 percent of the top positions in US corporations.[1] Somehow, women are being lost on their way up. Much has been written about women leaders; rarely do we hear them speak. Here you will hear from the women themselves.

The Lost Leaders in this book are women who share a life experience: they were part of the first wave of women who joined the corporate workplace en masse and moved up the ranks—only to eventually become so discouraged that they abandoned their careers. Although their stories are each unique, when viewed together, they provide a fascinating glimpse of the culture that exists in the contemporary corporation.

These Lost Leaders are not famous. They are just a few of the many women who were part of this major transition in our cultural history. Their anonymity makes them all the more interesting. No one was watching them, following them around, or praising their success. Their struggles were silent; they did it for themselves, their families, their companies. They began careers in the late 1970s and early 1980s, eager to climb the ladder to success. The women's movement gave them the opportunity to enter the business world as professional peers to men. Surely, many of them should have risen to the top by now. Instead, they were lost to the corporate world, choosing to leave it behind, some as early as 1998, others leaving well into the 2000s.

I am a member of this unwitting group. I graduated from college in 1977 and was recruited to join the largest accounting firm in the world. I thought my future was limitless. Being allowed into management, and eventually into the executive ranks, was not an opportunity that we took lightly. We needed to prove those brave activists of the 1970s were correct—that we were just as capable as men of succeeding by the harsh rules of business. Those rules were set long before women were allowed in, as was the culture of the workplace—what is valued, what behaviors are rewarded. We didn't try to change the game or its rules. We learned the rules and complied, even if the rules made no sense to us, even when complying meant denying a part of who we were, even when following all the rules, behaving like the successful men we saw around us, caused us to be labeled—but not as leaders. Somehow, emulating successful men was not only not enough to succeed, it backfired.

No one could tell us what behaviors were considered "acceptable" for women in business, but it was clear such things were not up to us to decide. They were always decided *by* men, *for* women. This fact is often ignored. We say it is "just business," the way American business operates. It is important to acknowledge the simple fact that the rules of business, and the very culture of business, were built around men, long before women entered the workplace, much less the executive suite. So far, women have only succeeded when they can figure out what works in this world that was not designed for them.

Given the seemingly impossible task of figuring out and practicing "appropriate" behaviors—which had to be done at the same time as the more practical task of learning the business itself and developing the competencies needed to succeed in management—it is miraculous that the career successes of the women in this book ever occurred. Strong economic times helped, creating opportunities for anyone who could "tough it out"—and work hard. These women were very hard workers, all dedicated to their careers, believing that a woman had to "be twice as smart and work twice as hard" as a man to achieve the same success. And many of us did succeed—beyond anything we could have imagined growing up.

In this book, representatives of the Lost Leaders reveal their personal stories and share their views about the business world where they thrived, at least for a time. Their stories were collected during my research for a PhD in applied anthropology. I wanted to look back, a decade after my own departure from the corporate world, with the perspective of someone who was there, but who also has the benefit of time away. My goal is to try to look objectively, as objectively as possible, as an anthropologist and feminist, at what happened (and is still happening) to women who could be leaders, but have chosen to "opt out."

In Part 1, Accidental Careers, the Lost Leaders introduce themselves. To understand this generation of women, it is important to consider how they came to find themselves in powerful positions in business. They certainly weren't raised with this expectation. At the time that most of us grew up, the career possibilities open to women who went to college were generally limited to teaching or nursing. The only women in corporations were secretaries. Some of those secretaries were college educated, but they rarely moved into executive roles. When the women's movement happened, the possibilities exploded, but there were no role models or examples of career paths for us to follow. In many ways these careers were "accidental." Each woman's path was unique—and unplanned. It is a unique snapshot of the dilemmas that face women in our society and lends context to the stories the Lost Leaders tell of corporate culture.

In Part 2, Corporate America, I have taken the stories the Lost Leaders told about their workplaces and grouped them around some common themes—topics that came up, again and again—in all of the interviews. I did not choose these topics; they came up spontaneously, as did the term "Corporate America," which the women use to label the culture of their workplaces. I asked each woman to tell me about the culture in the companies where she worked, and to share some stories to make it come alive. I provided a cursory definition of "corporate" culture, but encouraged the women to define it for themselves. My definition was: shared values and beliefs, traditions, what is important to the company and to its leaders, including things like dress codes and meetings, as well as language, how people treat one another, what sort of behaviors are acceptable, and which behaviors are rewarded. It is here that the Lost Leaders provide an insider's view of the inner workings of organizations, from the perspective of executives who were part of the leadership team, at least on paper. It is also here that we learn what caused them to be lost.

Despite what they experienced and their sense of loss from their abandoned corporate careers, the women still want to work and to utilize their talents. In Part 3, Hopes for the Future, they speak of their desire to work and tell how they have taken back the power to control their careers. They also share some of their ideas, possible solutions, for what needs to change so that women can stay and succeed. They are remarkably hopeful that the situation inside of corporations can change to allow the women who followed them in to succeed—and lead.

It has been said that we "blazed the trail," but that was not what it felt like while it was happening. It was just another day at the office, another challenge to turn into an opportunity, another slight to overlook, one more night to work late. It has also been said that we broke the "glass ceiling." If the ceiling has been broken, the stories told here reveal another floor above, another ceiling waiting. This book makes it clear that "blazing the trail" and "breaking the ceiling" are just empty expressions. There is not anything the Lost Leaders or the women who follow them can do to save their careers. The workplace has to change.

Although there has been tremendous change since the careers depicted here began, the environment that led these women to leave is still prevalent. I am continually confronted with situations that echo the stories here. For example, I was recently told of a young female engineer who graduated from a prestigious school. After tiring of the macho culture she found in engineering firms, she joined a mid-sized manufacturer, working on product patenting. Following her recent marriage, she was told by her male boss that "working moms don't get promoted here." She plans to join the ranks of the Lost Leaders soon.

Throughout this book, it is my goal to tell this story in the words of the Lost Leaders themselves. Their personal experiences illuminate today's workplace. It is my hope that those with the power to make change—the leaders who have not been lost—will listen to the voices of these women and begin to change the workplace now so that the Corporate America of tomorrow is truly led by the best and brightest, regardless of gender.

PART 1

Accidental Careers

In the 1950s, William H. Whyte, Jr. wrote "The Organization Man," and provided us with a description of the stereotypical business*man* of that era.[1] He is a *man,* of course, and conforms to a strict conservative code, assimilating easily into the office culture of the time. He will be loyal to one company his entire career and his loyalty will earn him job security and a gold watch, not to mention a nice pension plan, upon retirement.[2] The workplace was still dominated by these organization men when the Lost Leaders first began entering it in the late 1970s. By the 1990s, when they began to leave, the environment had changed dramatically; there is now little loyalty on the part of either the company or the employee. But the men still looked pretty much the same, and they still had no problem assimilating into cultures that were created by the organization men that came before them.

But what of the "organization woman?" Based on the Lost Leaders in this book, I offer this composite for the organization woman of the 1990s: Although she didn't grow up expecting to have a lofty title and earn a six-figure salary, she finds herself in a beautifully appointed corner office with a large staff reporting to her. She is highly educated, having earned an MBA at night while building her career. She is married with two children and is constantly challenged both by the logistics of a young family and the emotional energy it takes to hold down an executive position and raise children at the same time.

When I first met each Lost Leader, I asked her to tell me the story of her career. I grew up at roughly the same time, so I knew that we didn't set our sights on the "C-suite" as children. Somewhere during our childhood, when we learned that girls grew up to be wives, mothers, and sometimes teachers, the women's movement happened. We weren't quite old enough to participate in the movement, but it changed our lives and the lives of all women. Now we could have it all, or so we were told. These new options led the women in this book to become business professionals and eventually executives. None of them, and I'd venture few of this era, had this as her childhood dream.

In the next five chapters (chapters 1–5), the women describe how their paths led into business, how they became the executives whose careers took the turns that led them to be Lost Leaders. They also introduce us to the companies where they built their careers and to some of the "characters" that play significant roles in their stories. These stories give you a sense of who they are and what they might have contributed to the success of American businesses, if they had been given the opportunity and were not lost so early in their careers. Although some of the women stayed in business until they were in their fifties, their careers had been stalled much earlier by the obstacles they faced. Not all of those obstacles are the result of them being female in male-dominated workplaces. In some cases they chose not participate in the business practices and treatment of employees that they felt were not proper or ethical. Was their view of business ethics skewed by their being female? Possibly. Are there male executives who also objected? Certainly. The stories the women tell will reveal some of the culture and practices that led to ethical breaches that contributed to the crises in such companies as Lehman Brothers and Goldman Sachs. They are well worth listening to, as businesses try to rebuild their reputations. The women also tell of lingering sexism that haunted their careers.

Table P.1 may be useful as a reference to the Lost Leaders, their employers and their bosses, all of whom are given pseudonyms to protect their identities.

Table P.1 Lost Leaders background information

	Approximate year of birth	Career began in	Corporate employment ended in	Years in corporate	Highest position Held	Areas of expertise	Companies where employed (pseudonyms)	Type of Company
Barbara James	1959	1981	2003	22	Director	Finance	BGV	Telecom
Colleen Roberts	1951	1974	2005	31	Director	Marketing	Mercantile	Retail
Joyce Williams	1965	1987	1998	11	Director	Finance/Marketing	Insight / Top Tier / Goldstar	Software / Consumer Products / Regulated Industry
Judy Samuels	1951	1974	2001	27	Vice President	Human Resources	MegaBank	Financial Services
Mary Anne Josephson	1965	1987	1998	11	Director	Organizational Behavior	N/A	
Nancy Michaels	1959	1985	2004	19	Senior Vice President	Finance/Operations	Pollyanna	Entertainment
Patricia Alexander	1964	1987	2005	16	Vice President	Finance/Process Improvement	Comp Sales / Big Box	Technology / Retail
Pegge George	1959	1981	2003	22	Senior Manager	Engineering/Sales	EngineerInc / Consolidated	Industrial Products / Industrial Products
Susan Thomas	1949	1977	1998	21	Vice President	Sales/Quality	Mainstream Manufacturing	Consumer Products
Author	1954	1977	1993	16	Assistant Vice President	Accounting/Finance	N/A	
Average:	1958	1981	2001	20				

CHAPTER ONE

Colleen Roberts

Colleen is a strong woman, raised by a long line of strong women. Nearly six feet tall, she is slim and attractive, with short blond hair and a distinctive Southern drawl. When I met with her at her tastefully decorated home in an historic district, she served me iced tea and cookies using napkins that had been her mother's. If I had not come to interview her about her career, I would have assumed she was a Southern belle, not a hard-driving executive.

Colleen grew up in a small town in the South with conservative values, but the women around her taught her that she could be anything she wanted to be. This was highly unusual for the 1950s. Her strength was an advantage at times in her career, but in her last job it created problems with the men in leadership. She feels they were threatened by women in positions of authority. They thwarted her efforts to help their business grow. Eventually, this situation became untenable for both Colleen and the men in charge, and she joined the ranks of the Lost Leaders. Here she tells us a little about herself and the company that she left just a few days before I met her:

I was born in 1951, the youngest of three children. I grew up in the Deep South. The fortunate part of my upbringing is that I had a mother who was my role model, smartest woman I've ever known. She was a writer. She taught school, but her heart was in writing. She actually chose, after World War II, when everybody was having babies and staying home, my mother chose to go back to work. She did not want to stay home. It was a small town and she was a few blocks away; she never missed any of my piano concerts or any of that. It was obviously simpler times back then, the town was only 5,000 people; we could bicycle down the street and everybody knew us. We had nannies, black nannies that cooked and cleaned and took care of us.

My sister and I grew up thinking that was the way women are supposed to be, you are supposed to have your own life and find your own way, because my mother was very happy doing it. I was also influenced by my grandmother on my father's side. She lived in my hometown and she was also a schoolteacher. She was from a family of seven children. Six were girls and all six of those women went to college and all six of them taught school. When you got in a room with them, when they all got together on holidays, it was a little overwhelming, because these women were strong. My grandfather cooked the Christmas dinner every year; my grandmother didn't know how to cook. So I grew up in this environment of these women that were absolutely fabulous. I can remember as a child sitting around the card table with these old women. Loud, was it loud in there! They would stay up till one, two o'clock in the morning playing cards with us kids.

I was just fortunate to grow up around a lot of confident women that showed me at a very early age that your life is what you make it to be. Whatever you want to be, you are strong and you can do it. A great example was a conversation I had with my Mom when I was in the seventh grade. It was 1963. We always laughed about it later. It was when my brother graduated from high school and had been accepted at a major university. We were having dinner, talking about his going to college. My sister pipes up and says she wants to be a schoolteacher like my grandmother and great aunts. My mom looked at me and said, "What do you want to be?" I was 12, and I said, "I want to be Alex's secretary." I hadn't thought much about college and, at 12, I adored my brother. Wherever he was going, I wanted to go. So I said, "I'll work for Alex and I'll be his secretary." My mother looked at me across the table and she said, "You'll be what?" I said, "I'll work for Alex." She said, "Has it ever occurred to you that you could be a lawyer just like him? You could work in the same office with him, but you could be a lawyer." I will never forget that conversation. I said, "Okay, fine, I'll be a lawyer."

In college I got interested in market research, so I majored in marketing and went to work in advertising. After I graduated, I found a small agency and formed a good relationship with one of the senior account people and he took me under his wing. I never felt hindered by the male environment or the male executives there, because they were all brilliant, and I so respected what they were teaching me.

I met a gentleman who was with a large company and he got transferred to another city. We dated long distance for about a year and a half, then I moved to be with him and we got married. Then, like every big company executive, he got lured away by another corporation and we moved again. I was the dutiful wife and I didn't regret it. It was okay because I was in my early thirties and I felt like my career was really doing fine. For example, I got a chance to work with a creative team out of New York, and I actually did the advertising for the "Easy Bake" oven. I had one as a child, and I couldn't believe it; it was a thrill.

Eventually I got a job in a 60-year-old firm, one of the oldest advertising agencies in the Northeast. The four executives were stuffy old men. That was the first time I hit that environment. Here I was, young, in my thirties, so full of everything, just trying to build a résumé. I hit that agency, and I said, "I'm just going to have to teach them, because they're not doing it the way I was trained and I know what I'm doing is right." Needless to say, it was a rocky road at first. But in the third year I became the first female vice president in the history of that company, at the age of 35. But it was tough; it was hard. I felt so good that I was finally there. That's what I felt like in my mid-thirties. I had arrived.

Well, lo and behold, my husband decides he hates the city we were in and his new job. I didn't want to leave. I was making good money, loving my job. But we moved. That was about 20 years ago, around the mid-eighties. It took me quite a while to find a position that paid anything comparable to what I was making, due to a completely different job market in the Southeast. I ended up at a start-up agency that offered tremendous growth potential. For the next five years, I traveled almost three weeks a month. I loved it at first, but, after five years, I went to them and asked to be taken off the road. I was literally collapsing from all the travel. They said no, so I quit. Within two years they lost every piece of business that I had brought in and two years after that, the agency closed down. They lost it all.

This company certainly suffered by losing Colleen as a leader. She then went to work for a growing private company with a regional presence that I will call Mercantile, a pseudonym for this franchised retail operation. She stayed at Mercantile for the nine years prior to our interviews. During this time she also became divorced from the man that she had followed through all of his career moves.

The first six years at Mercantile were absolutely insane, crazy. I was working 70- and 80-hour weeks because I was building an internal advertising agency. It was such a great experience. When I joined that company, there was nothing in the way of advertising and marketing. They had no brand identity, they had no image, they had no PR, they had nothing. I was part of building all of it. But the environment at that company was very different from anything I'd ever seen. It was privately owned by a father and son, Mike Sr. and Mike Jr., who built it from scratch.

A couple years before I was hired, they hired a CFO. His name was Tim, and Mike's brother had been named Tim. That Tim, the oldest of Mike Sr.'s children, was killed by a drunk driver when he was 19. So here comes young Tim into the company. He ingratiated himself to Mike Sr., the owner. Mike Sr. calls him Timmy, which is the nickname he had for his son. Timmy can do no wrong; he is promoted in six years and is the first person to become of vice president in that company. He was the only person who had a title except Mike Sr. who was chairman and Mike Jr. who was president and CEO.

Well, I think Tim is the dumbest man in the world. I never got along with him, ever. He's the only person in my entire career who I ever looked at and said, "You are so full of shit. You don't know what you're talk-ing about," in front of six people. Later on I apologized to him and said, "That was very unprofessional," but I was so angry, because he constantly made comments in meetings I was chairing. I knew he didn't know what he was talking about; he was just trying to impress Mike Sr.

Tim and Steve, who was marketing director, have no vision for the com-pany. They know they want 200 stores. They consider that their vision, but that's just a goal. When I would sit in meetings with them and try to talk to them about what we need in customer service, why we need to train our store owners, the things that we need to do to make us a better business down the road—not a larger business, but a better business—they didn't want to hear it. I think it was partially because it was coming from a woman, and I think the second part of it is that Tim, being an accountant, could never justify the money for these programs. And I kept saying, "You've got to look outside the window. You've got to open that window, because we have a lot of competition now." The competitive environment had changed and I spent two years talking to them about the changes that I felt we needed. I tried to get them to let me solicit customer feedback. They don't want customer feedback.

Three years ago, Tim was promoted again, this time to executive vice president. I'm certain they gave him ownership in the company. At the same time they promoted the marketing director, Steve, who was hired six months after me, to vice president of marketing. The two of them were to lead this team into the future. I was overlooked.

Colleen's career success was significant, but her credentials were not enough to overcome an environment where the men seemed resistant to the opinions of a strong, outspoken woman. This appears to have come as something of a surprise to her, possibly because of the way she was raised, but also because of her earlier success and her positive experiences with men in the advertising business. Perhaps those were the outliers, or perhaps it was just poor leadership at Mercantile. Either way, she is now among the Lost Leaders, selling real estate in the small town where she grew up.

Like Colleen, many of the Lost Leaders had positive experiences with male mentors during their careers. Their success probably would not have occurred without them. This might have been part of why these women lasted as long as they did, and why some of them were caught off guard when they hit the now infamous "glass ceiling" or had a run-in with what they call the "old boy network."

A few of the other Lost Leaders share Colleen's experience of being a "trailing spouse." As more women have moved up into executive ranks, couples struggle to balance the needs of two powerful careers. Barbara and Pegge, who will be introduced later, found their own careers stalled because they were not willing to accept transfers that would disrupt their families. Women continue to be more likely to be the ones who sacrifice career success for that of their husbands, partially because the men are still more likely to be at higher levels of responsibility with larger salaries, but also because traditional roles and societal norms are often more difficult to break than glass ceilings.

CHAPTER TWO

Judy Samuels

Judy Samuels was certainly not destined for the business world. Graduating from high school in 1968, she was encouraged to choose a traditionally female career and ended up as a secretary in a bank. She set herself the goal of becoming a loan officer but, along the way, she found her true calling: human resources. Her story provides a unique benefit to this discussion of Lost Leaders because she was directly involved in the corporate diversity movement at a major corporation. Judy's love of human resources came more from her competitive instinct than any need to nurture. She loved the "hunt" of finding the right person for each job and the challenge of transforming a corporate culture.

Judy worked at essentially the same company for 25 years, through its rapid growth and numerous mergers. She eventually reached the executive ranks of "MegaBank," which was then one of the largest financial services firms in the United States. When I interviewed her about five years later, she still held a bitter viewpoint of what had happened at the end of her career:

My parents were working people, putting my brother through college at a state university. He was allowed to go away, although I was a better student. Back then, believe it or not, you were a teacher, a nurse, or an airline stewardess. I soon realized that I didn't want to do any of those three things. I really didn't know what I wanted to do, so I went to junior college, got my AA degree and decided I was going to start working. I decided to try being a secretary because in high school I took shorthand and typing, at my mother's suggestion. That was a good job at the time, but I very quickly learned that was not a place I wanted to be long-term. I did not want to be a secretary.

There was a job advertised in the paper for secretary for the president of a bank. My thinking at the time was, "If I can get in there, I can get into a training program." They hired me as the assistant to the president, a wonderful job, great opportunity. That's where I really learned the guts of banking. I went to all the board meetings, loan committee meetings, the audit committee meetings. It was just very interesting and eye opening. That is where the light bulb went on, and I said, "I'm going back to school. I'm going to get my degree in accounting and finance. I'm going to be a banker." I went to school at night, because I was working full-time. During those years I had my eyes set on going into the lending area because that's where my professors were telling us the money was. There weren't a lot of women in that arena.

This was around 1980 or 1981, and I approached the personnel director about their credit training program, and he said to me, "Listen, we have a lot of problems here in personnel. If you come and help us, I promise you I'll put you in the training program later." That training was really exactly what I wanted, because that was a way that I could get on the line and become a lender. So I went into the personnel group.

Listening to Judy tell her story today, it seems odd that she would accept such a big diversion in her career goal. She apparently felt she was doing the company a favor and that it would earn her a place in the training program she wanted. Now it can easily be seen as a ploy to appease her in hope that she would accept a more traditionally female part of the business, personnel, instead of rocking the boat by trying to be a lender where, she admits, there were few women. Planned or not, the ploy worked.

I really loved it. It was really fun, and I got better at it. I liked talking to different kinds of people. I loved the hunt and I loved filling the jobs. I was asked if I would do the management side, after just six months. My boss said, "You are still going to go into the credit training program, maybe next year." I went to bat for them and I said, "I can do that training program anytime."

The bank I worked for was small, privately owned, and very entrepreneurial; people really helped one another. I knew each of them well. There wasn't a hierarchy. There was leadership, but people called each other by their first names. It was just a great environment, a wonderful place to learn. In 1986 our small bank was sold to a large national bank. That was the first time that I got exposure to what acquisitions or mergers were all about. The bank continued to grow and I took on more responsibility, and soon it just flourished and grew with more acquisitions, more mergers. I was asked in 1996 to be director of human resources for the entire state. I had to move to a different city, where I didn't know a soul. That was a very big eye-opener for me, after being very cocooned, living most of my life in the city where I was born and raised.

Then there were seven mergers in five years, the last one creating what is now MegaBank. That last merger was very much a turning point, in terms of the way the organization was run. Just before that, I was asked to be in charge of all of the human resources in the largest division, a vice president position. I was asked to move back to my hometown, which was a blessing for me. I moved back here in 1999 and in February of 2000 the merger was announced. That merger really became very difficult. A lot of individuals were consolidated, lost their jobs. Thousands of people in the organization and many at the higher end, their jobs were eliminated or moved, or they took early retirement.

The people that I considered my mentors, the top leaders in the company, were asked to leave and I knew that the organization was changing. There was a different way of treating people and I just didn't want to be part of that any more. I chose to ask my boss to have my job eliminated, because I wanted severance. I didn't want to move to the new headquarters. It was a new organization then and I just felt it was the right time for me to leave.

So I took my two years of severance and went home. I had never had a résumé in my life and never intended to work anywhere else. All of my networking was halted, because everything that I did in working some 70 plus hours a week was geared towards the bank. I had to really take a walk on the beach. When I cut my wrists and saw what was inside, it was green and gold, the logo colors of MegaBank. I needed to get my own blood back. I had been with them for 27 years. I had the mindset that I was going to be with the bank until I retired. When I left I was 50, I hadn't really thought about plan "B." I only had plan "A." Looking back, it was a scary time, but it was also such a freeing time. I was very confident that I was going to land somewhere, I just didn't know where.

Her severance package, combined with future retirement benefits that she had earned, left Judy financially independent, but she was not ready to retire. She took some time to reflect on what she really wanted to do with her life and eventually found her plan "B," starting her own business as an executive recruiter. She has a business partner but no office, no staff, and no bosses.

One of the things that I love is that I don't have to deal with any of the politics. I don't have to deal with any of the superfluous, nonsensical, ridiculous conference calls and meetings that don't add any value and are very ego driven. Everything that I do is based on adding value.

I would say that I picked myself up, dusted myself off, and, with luck and good graces from above, things have really worked out. I love what I am doing. I'm happier than I have ever been.

Judy is a great example of what happens to many women when they lose their corporate careers. Although men sometimes struggle with the loss of identity that Judy faced at first, women often take the loss as an opportunity for soul searching and find new work that they really love. My friends and I always joke that when the men we worked with were laid off they went into a depression, while when we got a severance package we threw a party.

Judy does not mind at all that she no longer has the title and perks that come with being a corporate executive. All of the women here have made this transition to some extent. Although they may be Lost Leaders to the corporate world, they still want to work. They are not ready to give up the satisfaction they gain from using the skills they developed in their work lives.

Like Colleen, Judy never had children. None of the four women here who were over 50 at the time of the interviews had children. They were also single during most of their corporate careers, three being divorced early and one not marrying until after she turned 50. The younger women included in this book began their careers a few years later and managed to marry and have children along the way. Marriage and children, however, added to their challenges, as we will see in their career stories.

CHAPTER THREE

Joyce Williams

Joyce is the youngest woman in this book. An attractive blond, married to a successful real estate developer, and living with their two beautiful young children in her dream home, she would appear to be the epitome of the country-club wife. Joyce is anything but. She was born to be an entrepreneur, but she decided to start out in the corporate world to gain some practical experience. Once there, she was caught up in the high of her own rapid success. In only eleven years she achieved more than many people do in a full career—but she still had a dream, and a grievance. Her dream was to be self-employed; her grievance was the environment that operates in corporations, particularly how challenging it is to find work–life balance. She took action on both her dream and her grievance, growing two successful businesses and coauthoring a book on work–life balance. Along the way, she experienced a rapidly growing high-tech company, a highly structured *Fortune* 50 monolith, and a regulated industry struggling to learn the competitive model. Beginning her career at 22 in 1987 and exiting her last corporate job in 1998 at only 33, her story is almost too much to believe, and these are just the highlights:

I originally wanted to go to school for landscape architecture but my parents talked me out of it, saying, "You'll never work!" They have that depression-era mentality. They thought that if you major in business, you can always get a job. I ended up majoring in marketing, because that was the more creative end of the business school, and minoring in finance.

I knew, even before I started working for a company, that I intended to be an entrepreneur someday. My father is an attorney and has his own practice. My mom, once I was in high school, became a real estate agent. So, for all intents and purposes, they are fairly entrepreneurial. I'm sure some of my interest in owning a business was because of their advice to "control your own destiny." I went into Corporate America to get marketing experience, finance experience, sales experience. I felt, if I was going to have my own company someday, I would need those.

I started out working for a very small technology consulting company. It literally was five people. Every month we weren't sure whether we were going to make payroll, so it was very stressful, though I was learning a ton. Within six months I took my limited experience and went to a larger technology company, Insight, in their new consulting division. The whole company was $250 million in sales at that point, which is small for the IT industry. By the time I left, two and half years later, they were a 2.5 billion-dollar company—huge growth. It was an exciting time to be there because they were growing so rapidly you could create your own opportunities.

Then the company wanted all of the finance people back at their headquarters and, while I would have loved to move there, I was in the middle of grad school at the time at a top program. Through grad school, I met some colleagues that were at Top Tier, a Fortune 50 company in the area. They let me know there was a financial analyst position open, so I made the switch there. I was on the financial track. I was an analyst, and then a senior analyst, then my job got upgraded to a finance manager job. My manager then said, "Look around to see what job you want next, which director job do you want to go for when it opens up?" I looked around at all of them and I thought, "I don't really want any of these jobs. I feel like I know what I want to know from the financial side of the business." I also knew, at Top Tier, marketing runs the show. You run a business there if you are in marketing. It was an opportunity to basically go learn how to run a business with this giant safety net under me.

Switching from finance to marketing is not a common career path. They don't promote moving across job functions, but you can do it. I certainly wasn't the only one, but I was one of the very few that did it. Typically, people who are good at finance are not the same ones who do well in marketing. I was able to do both, and the marketing people respected me. That made it easier; I had them to campaign on the other side of the camp for me. Eventually, I was an associate brand manager for an entire product line.

Joyce admits that she is unusual in that she could do both finance and marketing, but leaves out the fact that she made this abrupt move mid-career and it didn't slow her meteoric rise up the corporate ladder. Her talents were recognized by Top Tier, but she still considered them too bureaucratic to hold her interest for long.

Mark, my mentor at Top Tier, moved to a new company, Goldstar, which was part of a regulated business, telecommunication, that was going through huge changes at the time. They were trying to deregulate the industry and needed to bring in people who had worked in competitive environments like ours to teach this very slow, plodding company how to compete. So I followed him there. Then my division was reorganized and I got a new position that was considered the plum job of the division. I mean literally, the division president made a point to say, "You're it. This is the best job." It was a director level position, responsible for moving the company away from a product focus mentality to a customer focus mentality. They were breaking the customer base into different segments and I was in charge of the customers that were considered the cream of the crop.

My group was told to "Go off and figure out what we should do and how we should promote our product and then come back and tell us." So we did. We spent quite a bit of time and came back with our recommendations. The management team basically responded, "No, that's not it. Go back" [laughs]. There were no criteria; it was like throwing a dart at a dart board. I finally said, "There is no way to succeed in this job. There literally is no way to succeed in it." They didn't know what they needed, which is why they hired me, but they wouldn't accept my recommendations. I also knew I was going to be out of there in a year anyway, regardless of whether I'm in the plum job or not. First of all, it wasn't the job I wanted, nobody ever bothered to ask me. I was working for a terrible manager; I had a terrible commute. It all finally coalesced—I always wanted to be on my own, but I had forgotten about it. I always thought, "Someday, someday, someday."

I ended up enjoying working for companies and being more successful than I ever thought I would. I always just had this idea that I was going to go out on my own and have my own business. But it's like anything; anytime you get into a company there is a tendency, you don't want to say you were co-opted, but in order to get the job done you have to get to know what the culture is, and you get caught up in that culture of succeeding and getting to the next level. Up until this point I had been learning so much and getting promoted. I was also getting more and more money, so there was the compensation that was hard to leave, but there was also the aggravation factor. I finally realized it was time. I didn't even bother talking to my current boss. I went to Mark, my mentor who brought me over from Top Tier, and I told him, "It's not Goldstar. The company clearly has issues, and I think there's going to be real problems here, but the reality is, it's time. It's time for me to move on and do my own thing."

Joyce started her new life by buying a local coffee shop. Eventually she expanded it to add a marketing business, selling gift baskets to corporations to use in their marketing efforts. Both businesses did well very quickly, but she eventually sold them when she had the opportunity to pursue another dream, writing a book. Her book, about work–life balance, was picked up by a major publisher and kept her busy, for a few years, with speaking engagements and seminars, while also allowing her to realize a very personal goal, starting a family.

Although Joyce experienced some blatant discrimination during her career, which she will share later, she never lacked for opportunities. She was continually moving up, even when she chose to change companies or even careers, moving from finance to marketing in midstream. Her competence was recognized and rewarded, yet she always knew she would control her own destiny. She attributes this to her parents' entrepreneurial nature, but a large part of her decision was based on her desire to have children. Perhaps because she is one of the youngest Lost Leaders, or perhaps just because she is Joyce, she was not willing to accept some of the things that she observed older women accepting. The most significant thing she was not willing to compromise was her vision of parenting. She could not reconcile it with the demands of the corporate workplace.

CHAPTER FOUR

Nancy Michaels

Nancy came of age at the height of the women's movement of the 1970s. Her story is not that of an activist, but she was certainly a nonconformist and her career had the most unlikely of beginnings. It typifies the "accidental" nature of the careers of women of this generation. I never met Nancy in person, only over the telephone. In her interviews, she did not sound like the high level executive that she was. We might expect her to speak in a polished and professional manner, but the culture of the company where she achieved most of her success was one that accepted, maybe even valued, fighting and cursing, a true "boys" club. She speaks very matter-of-factly, sometimes even crudely. She also has some interesting perspectives to share about what actually goes on inside the executive suite. Despite its rocky start, her career led her to the very top of the corporate hierarchy, just one chair away from the presidency of a *Fortune* 100 company. What she found there eventually led her to abandon her tremendous success.

I left home when I was about 16, just after my junior year of high school. It was sort of in the wild days, post-Vietnam. I have an older brother and an older sister and I think they wore my parents out. I told them I was going away for the weekend, and I didn't come back. I moved in with my boyfriend who had gone to college. I always credit my parents. A lot of parents would force you to come back, or call the police. My parents, I think they were tired. It was different back then, they decided to *let go. That was probably the best thing that could have happened to me, because I grew out of being a snotty, selfish, obnoxious teenager into someone who realizes that you have to work to pay the bills and feed yourself. It was a maturing experience. I found a lady who was willing to help me get a job as a nurse's aide. I lived with my boyfriend for the better part of three years and worked in a nursing home, worked multiple jobs and had to wash my clothes by hand and hang them outside and do all those things that you have to do when you're making $2.50 an hour.*

Eventually I moved back to my hometown and broke up with the boyfriend. I was on my own, working at a factory. That job didn't pay enough to actually live on, so I was working also at a pizza place and at a gas station. The gas station I was working for, back in the days when they actually pumped gas, lost a supervisor. They asked me if I wanted to be a supervisor, which I had never thought about. I was all of 18. I thought, "Sure, what the heck?" I started working full-time and then the manager quit and they asked me if I wanted to be a manager, and I said, "Sure, what the heck?" I was managing a gas station where the employees were 18-year-old boys, and that was interesting. I was definitely the "Attila the Hun" kind of manager; I think that's what most people do when they start. But it was a good company that sent new managers to their headquarters to a management training program, so I actually started to learn about management.

I wanted to go back to school, but I didn't know what I wanted to do. I was going to weekend culinary school, I was working at a restaurant, and I started taking at the same time (when I think about the energy I had at that age!) classes at the local community college, business classes. Eventually, I transferred to a university to get an accounting degree. I just decided, "Oh, accounting is something I am good at."

Actually, right about that time, my father, who was president of an insurance company and had been in the insurance business for years, got fired. It was pretty devastating. That was right in the 80s when a lot of people were losing their jobs. That made me want to find something that would provide a lot of security. I thought that in accounting, you can hang out your own shingle; you can work in public accounting or in a corporation. I thought it sounded like a good idea. That's how I stumbled into it.

Up to this point, Nancy's career trajectory was almost entirely accidental, but now she joins the ranks of the top accounting graduates as they begin their careers in what were then known as the "Big 8," the largest and most prestigious accounting firms. She shares this early career experience with two of the other Lost Leaders, who will be introduced in the next chapter. Accounting seems to be a place where many women felt comfortable entering the business world, perhaps because the field included a large number of clerical positions. Although the big firms were hiring many women, it was not without trepidation on their part. I recall a quote from the managing partner of one of the big firms from about this time. He said that if he hired only the top grads from accounting programs he would be hiring *only* women, but in two years he would not have anyone to promote to the next level. He, like many business leaders, still believed that women were only planning to work until they found husbands or started families. Since he and his contemporaries did nothing to change their workplaces to be hospitable to women or to accommodate those with family responsibilities, much of what he predicted came true. But Nancy, and the two other Lost Leaders who started in the Big 8, persevered in the corporate workplace decades longer than he predicted.

From college I made the decision to go into public accounting. I was with a large CPA firm for four years and fast tracked through their roles, making it to a supervisor/manager position. Then I decided to get out into real businesses, rather than be an auditor. My parents had moved to a warmer climate then so, sort of on a lark, I sent a résumé to Pollyanna Entertainment, a large company near them. Pollyanna was eager to hire CPAs from the big accounting firms. I started working as a supervisor and worked through several supervisor and manager roles in accounting, and ultimately went to operational finance, which is what started to expand my career.

That corporate experience was certainly a good one, for the work experience anyway. The people, from a colleague standpoint, were nice, but Pollyanna was not at all a "Pollyanna" place from a management standpoint.

Nancy's reference to "Pollyanna" here implies that although the outward appearance of the company is that it is a pleasant, nurturing place—somewhere children will be happy—the management culture was very different from that outward appearance.

I was trying to get out of Pollyanna for a couple of years, and finally a good opportunity came along at a Fortune *100 company nearby, Comp Sales. While I was at Comp Sales I got my masters in an executive MBA program. It was not about the learning, I'm afraid to say. I knew being female, I had that hurdle, if you will, and I didn't want to have to make excuses for my résumé. I wanted to have everything that everybody else had, whose résumés are going in front of them, when I came up for promotions. I told my boss that I wanted to go to school and he was hemming and hawing about whether I could manage it, and I felt, "Give me a break!" It was every other Friday, minimal time away from the office. Of course I had to make every promise in the world that I would keep on working a million hours. I completed the MBA when my daughter was seven or eight months old. My husband was a stay-at-home dad and one of the good things about that is it's easier to juggle, because you have a second set of hands.*

I started at Comp Sales as a director in accounting, was promoted to controller, eventually vice president and eventually senior vice president. It was a high point financially and responsibility-wise in my career, senior vice president for a Fortune *100 company and I was an officer of the company, at 47 years old.*

In part 2, Nancy will share more stories of the culture she found in this major corporation and the events that led her to resign. She will also describe her attempts to create a different type of culture at Comp Sales. One question that continues to bother many women is why the women before them did not change the environment for the better. Nancy's experience will provide some illumination on the subject. Her story is particularly interesting because, not only did she not become part of the established environment, she was not left jaded by her experience. She remains optimistic that things will change for the better, as she shares in part 3.

Nancy's family structure, with a stay-at-home dad, is a cultural shift brought about as part of the success of this generation of female executives. Because companies have not changed from a model that assumes executives have wives to tend to household matters, many early women entrants to this level did not marry or have children, whether by choice or coincidence. As younger women arrived, one adaptation is for the husband to either stay at home or take a less demanding job than his wife, to provide that "second set of hands," usually contributed by wives of executives. Although this might be viewed as a movement toward more equality, men willing to take on nurturing roles, it also keeps businesses from having to change and demonstrates the resilience of the ideal worker ideology that will be discussed in part 2.

CHAPTER FIVE

Other Lost Leaders

Pegge George

Pegge is the only Lost Leader in this book with a degree in engineering. Despite having such a highly marketable degree, she did not build her career in engineering, a field in which women are still very much in the minority. At the time she attended college, Pegge would have been one of only a handful of women in her classes. She quickly made the decision not to pursue what she terms "real" engineering but was able to use her technical knowledge to build a career in sales for manufacturing companies. Although she did not elaborate on that decision, it seems likely that being so much in the minority in the ranks of the "real" engineers played a role. Pegge also has a very pleasant, open personality, a trait that served her well in sales but may have been a detriment in the more masculine world of engineering. Pegge worked for large corporations, EngineerInc and Consolidated Manufacturing, which were subject to strict affirmative action regulations. Although she does not believe she benefitted from affirmative action, these companies were always very anxious to offer her the next step-up. Despite this, her career stalled because she was not willing to relocate once her husband became a company president. She also struggled to limit her business travel. It was the travel that eventually led her to leave the corporate workplace. She was tired of trying to balance her travel with that of her husband's and the needs of their young children. Pegge started a consulting practice, which gives her the flexibility she needs to balance her family and work lives.

Patricia Alexander

Patricia made a decision to go into business when she was only 12 years old. When her parents got divorced, she watched her mother struggle and their standard of living decline. She was determined that she would always be financially independent. She earned a double major in accounting and finance and started her career at a large accounting firm. She left after just three years because she wanted to start a family and did not feel that the work schedule required in that business was compatible with parenting. The company where she spent most of her career, and which she speaks of here, is a large regional retail organization we will call Big Box. Beginning on the professional staff in the finance area in 1990, she progressed quickly and eventually was the director of a large group of internal consultants. She was involved in all aspects of the business and reported directly to the president. But management changes led Patricia and this prestigious group to be devalued and she never reached the vice president level at Big Box. She also struggled, as she will share in part 2, with what she terms a "face time" culture. Living far from her office and raising children, she had difficulty meeting the expectations of some who felt she needed to spend more time physically in the office. She left to pursue commercial real estate as an independent broker where she has more flexibility and can work closer to home.

Mary Anne Josephson

Mary Anne built her career in the still relatively new field of human resources. No longer just the "personnel" folks who handle hiring and payroll, these professionals study organizational behavior and strive to make people-intensive businesses more effective. Mary Anne parlayed this expertise into her own consulting practice, where she works primarily as an executive coach. This role consists of being a sounding board and advisor to executives, not for making decisions about their products and services, but for dealing with other people, managing and navigating this thing called corporate culture. Her work provides Mary Anne with a unique viewpoint that, along with her years in corporate human resources, provides a wide-ranging picture of workplace culture. Her perspective includes insights from coaching other women in executive positions.

Barbara James

Barbara stumbled into business when her original career choice, dental hygienist, was abandoned after one semester of college chemistry. She found accounting more her style and, luckily, was at a large mid-Western university with an excellent business school. Upon graduation in 1981, she was recruited by a major corporation I will call BGV. There she was given the opportunity to be part of a management development program, working in three different six-month assignments before making a commitment to a locale or division of the company. The Latin American division intrigued Barbara. She had lived in South America as a child, until her father's untimely death when she was only eight, and she was fluent in Spanish. On her way up the career ladder, Barbara earned an MBA going to school at night and accepted an assignment in BGV's New York headquarters. There she had exposure to top executives, but also to high-level corporate politics and a more conservative business environment. A few years after they relocated her to a smaller city in the South, the company asked her move back to headquarters. She declined because she had just met the man that would soon become her husband. He was divorced with shared custody of a young child; moving was not an option. Barbara managed to land another good assignment, but knew that declining the headquarters position would limit her career potential. She had achieved the level of director, but would not move further up. She eventually left to begin a consulting business after her division was sold. After the sale, the culture of the organization devolved as the new management allowed an environment of drinking and partying to take over. Two years later, she has a growing consulting business and no regrets.

Susan Thomas

Susan was a liberal arts major whose first job after college was as a buyer in a department store. In 1977, at the age of 28, she was recruited into a management-training program at a major corporation, Mainstream Manufacturing. She believes that she was "a diversity hire," for this company—a beneficiary of affirmative action. When she was higher up in the organization she had access to information that identified a corporate goal of having three women in management. There was a financial incentive offered to see that it happened. Susan progressed through a series of challenging career positions, evolving from sales to marketing to quality management, while also completing her MBA. Susan's career required extensive travel. She enjoyed this when she was younger, but later, when she met her husband, she wanted a more normal life. In 1998, she took control of her own destiny and started a consulting business. She has built a professional reputation and manages to find plenty of work without ever getting on an airplane. Now that her practice is thriving, Susan says that self-employment means you get to pick which 23 hours a day you work, and she admits that she has not had a vacation since her honeymoon over five years ago. Despite the hours, and although she has had many attractive offers, she has resolved never to return to traditional employment.

Author

My career has many similarities to those of the other women featured here. I did not expect to go into business, although my father was a small business owner. I worked in his grocery store as a teen and watched him "do the books" at home every evening. My parents encouraged me to go to college, but my initial plan was to major in nursing, one of the more traditionally female roles. An early marriage delayed my plans. By the time I found my way to college, I knew I needed a career where I could support myself; I did not want to be dependent on a man. I started college as an engineering major but, having had very little prior exposure to sciences, I struggled with the coursework and I was not willing to take the time to catch up. I transferred to accounting, attracted by the growing number of women there as well as the lucrative starting salaries. I graduated in 1977 and spent the next six years in a Big 8 firm where I was often the only woman in the room and the culture was certainly male dominated. I learned to read the sports page so I would have something to talk about at lunch and to play a little golf and drink scotch—all of those things that many women struggled with at the time, trying to fit in but knowing that we really didn't. I also spent six years as a division controller at a growing insurance company. Again, I was almost always the only woman on the management team. There I had the opportunity to be an active member of a small group that was guiding a new division. My disillusionment with business began there, however, when our division, although extremely profitable, failed to grow as fast as the corporation desired. My boss, the division president, and my best friend in the company, the head of marketing, were fired and our division was left to flounder for several months. Eventually a new president came in and our division began to grow rapidly. Despite now meeting all of our goals, we were asked to eliminate 10 percent of our staff as part of a nation-wide "downsizing." I could not support that decision, so took it as my opportunity to get severance—and downsized myself. That was the end of my "corporate" career, but I continued in business with my own company, a staffing business that I started, grew and sold over a seven year period in the 1990s. It was after that experience that I turned to community work and decided to pursue a PhD in anthropology. Although going from being a CPA to being an anthropologist is quite uncommon (as far as I know I am the only one, ever) it makes perfect sense (to me, at least) in the context of the evolution of my career.

PART 2

Corporate America

Every workplace has its own nuances; some would say each has its own culture. Reading the stories told by the Lost Leaders together reveals an over-arching culture in the American workplace. The women refer to this as "Corporate America." There are many different companies, industry sectors, and cities represented here, yet a few topics came up over and over in my interviews with these former business executives. Those topics form the basis for the chapters in this section (chapters 6–10).

Though culture is often considered the domain of anthropology, not even anthropologists can agree on its definition. Culture within companies, often referred to as "corporate culture," cannot be separated from the larger culture, "American culture," which is even more difficult to define. In this book, I am considering corporate culture to be comprised of what is important to the leaders in a company, what is valued, including how people treat one another, what sort of behaviors are acceptable, and what behaviors are rewarded. I recognize that this is a simplification of the concept of culture, but consider it appropriate for the discussion here.

The Lost Leaders' stories were analyzed using feminist theory for the discussion in my dissertation. The women don't use the same words as the feminist theorists, but it was interesting to see how the stories they told fit with the theories and concepts of the academics. One concept, "hegemonic masculinity," was particularly apparent in their career stories. Applied to business, this concept means that most workplaces and business leaders are so entrenched in the male-dominated structure, viewing everything from a male viewpoint, that they have difficulty even making sense of women executives. Although women have been allowed in, they are still viewed as outsiders—different from the norm.[1] This concept pervades the discussion in the first two chapters here (chapters 6 and 7), The Old Boys' Network and The Acceptable Band.

Joan Williams, Director of the Center for WorkLife Law at the University of California Hastings, studies gender in the work-place. She has written extensively about the impact on women of the expectation by businesses that all employees function as "ideal workers," available around the clock and able to travel and relocate for the benefit of the business.[2] This concept provides the title for the third chapter in this section (chapter 8), The Ideal Worker. Several of the Lost Leaders exited their careers because of this expectation. Although it is clear they find this disappointing, they accepted it as just part of the job and found it difficult to suggest solutions. At some point, even these women became so entrenched in the current business model that it is not surprising that they have difficulty imagining a fundamentally different way of organizing work.

In chapter 9, Against the Law, the Lost Leaders tell stories of blatant discrimination. The fact that blatant discrimination per-sists provides evidence of the taken-for-granted system of sex roles in society and in business. This system often overcomes the logic of the law and makes discrimination more difficult to remedy.

Fast Company magazine once proclaimed American businesses "toxic places to work."[3] The Lost Leaders would not disagree. Chapter 10, The Toxic Workplace, provides a glimpse into what it is like to be at an executive level in American business, for both women and men. This played a large part in why these leaders were lost to the corporate world. Women entering into the upper echelons of these institutions may have begun to reshape them, but culture changes slowly, too slowly for this group. Some felt that the environment was actually getting worse, due to competitive pressures to grow and increase profits.

The personal stories of the Lost Leaders reveal how they experienced Corporate America and what eventually drove them out. Although they tend to have positive outlooks on life and are proud of their accomplishments, the tone of the women's stories here is decidedly negative. They accomplished more than they had ever imagined, but each left the corporate workplace before achieving her full potential. These stories reveal their frustrations and provide a critique of the businesses in which they spent, on average, 25 years of their lives.

CHAPTER SIX

The Old Boys' Network

As the women's stories begin to unfold, a term they use often is "the old boys' network:"

Through the years, there were many occasions where it's very clear that the good old boy, even though they're young professional men [laughs], the good old boy mentality is alive and well. And it's frustrating. (Nancy Michaels)

Much of the frustration stems from the fact that the "old" boys are young; another generation has joined the "club." At times, the women attempt to limit their remarks about the old boys' network to the industries in which they had personal experience. However, the stories of all the women here included similar comments, despite the fact that there are many different organizations and industries represented, indicating that this atmosphere is pervasive within American businesses. For example:

It was still very much a good old boys network. It was an engineering environment and women hadn't really gotten into it.

Public accounting, especially some of the big firms, were still by far kind of good old boy networks.

In general the paper industry is very good old boy.

There's very much a boys' club in real estate.

Although one might hope that this environment was a relic of the past, it appears in even the most recent stories. Its continued existence was supported in a story told recently by a friend who works in a large professional services firm that is often cited in the media as a good place to work for women. She told me that, as part of an employee survey, they asked women what their firm could do to improve its working environment. The most common answer was as follows: "get rid of the old boy network."

This "network," sometimes referred to as "boys' clubs," is not only an attitude; there are actual places and events where women are not welcome. Nancy expressed her amazement at this, which was still happening in 2003 when she left her position as a senior vice president at Comp Sales:

The whole golf course thing just makes me laugh. It's one of the things that haven't changed very much. Back in the 60s it was the gentleman's club and today it's the golf course or in some, surprising to me, even nice companies, it's the strip club. I find it kind of astounding and I'm not really a prude but I find the whole strip club phenomenon sort of amazing—that they didn't see the inappropriateness of something like that.

Mary Anne recalled an episode of *The Today Show* that dealt with this behavior:

The CEO of a company racked up like $240,000 at a strip club in New York City and it was for a client he was entertaining. The Today Show brought out some consultants to interview and asked them: "Is this what business is coming to now?" and "How are women supposed to compete when this is what is going on?" One guest commentator, a man, said, "You know, bottom line, I don't care how my people get results; they just need to get results." While the woman guest said, "This is not ethical." A male client is never going to ask a woman to take him to the strip club and spend money all night. How is she going to develop relationships and get results, if this is the way that relationships are promoted?

Judy expressed frustration with boys' clubs and does not think that women in power can change them:

A lot of things have been written about where business is done and we all know a lot of business is done on the golf course and a lot of business is done in the evening. If you are a female that has a family or a spouse or significant other or you don't play golf, you're out! I don't think that women are allowed to change it. It's like a creed, like smoking a cigar—not once have martinis been introduced into the boardroom. No, it's still the scotch, the cigars, and the dirty jokes.

At one point I worked for one of the highest-ranking female executives in the company and in our industry. I definitely think that it helped to have a few women that really were equal to or ahead of some of their male counterparts. It was very interesting to see people step up and really respect them or be totally intimidated by them. But I don't think that women who move up are allowed to change the culture. I think that's part of the reason why my boss never got on the board of directors, part of the reason why she didn't continue to move up. They don't want someone to rain on their parade. To break the rules of a male-dominated corporation is very, very, very difficult.

I certainly encountered my share of scotch, cigars, and dirty jokes, as well as my coworkers visiting strip clubs while working for a CPA firm. I also encountered an even more blatant example of exclusion—the men's luncheon club. Business lunches took place every day at private clubs that specifically excluded women. Nothing untoward was happening in these clubs, as far as I know, but the "members" just didn't feel that women belonged. When the subject came up, men would laugh and say things like, "Women talk too much," or "Their voices are too shrill," to explain why we couldn't join. The partners of the firm that I worked for owned a membership in just such a club, which occupied the top floor of the building where our offices were located. One of my most vivid memories of that time in my career is a day of meetings with a client who was visiting from England. I was assigned as senior manager on the engagement, but when it got to be lunchtime, the partner I was working with turned to me nonchalantly and said, "I am taking take Mr. Smith to lunch at the club, so you know that excludes you." He didn't say "I'm sorry," or even give it a second thought. I had been in meetings all morning with this partner and the client, and had spent days preparing for his visit, but I was not to be included at lunch.

I have to confess that I was not really looking forward to having lunch with these two men, but that is not the point. The point is that I was the manager and it was inappropriate for the partner to exclude me. A year or so later, when I resigned from the firm, the same partner took me to lunch (not to the club, of course!) and asked me if there were any issues that he and the other partners should know about—an informal exit interview. I reminded him of his lunch with the client from England. He didn't even remember it and seemed genuinely shocked that I had a problem with the firm having a membership in a club that excluded women. It was a normal part of his world and he had never questioned it. Eventually, all of the luncheon clubs in that town were opened to women. Along the way, one opened specifically to counter the practice of excluding women. When I returned to the same city in 1993 to start a business, guess which one I joined?

A more hidden example of a "boys' club" was described by Patricia who told stories from two different companies where the culture valued working in the office on weekends, a behavior she refers to as "face time."

I just felt like it was a boy's club. They went in there on Saturday morning and hung out and shot the shit for a few hours. They didn't really get any work done; it was just part of the club. Several of the top managers were always there. I wasn't going to waste my Saturday that way. But then, I wasn't part of that club, nor did I want to be. I found it distasteful that you have to give up your Saturday to be in the club.

These "clubs," whether they be separate physical spaces or behavior on the inside of workplaces, help to perpetuate the "good old boy" nature of business and exclude women from important relationships. Sometimes the women are invited, as Patricia was certainly "invited" to come to the office on Saturday morning, but they chose not to participate. In other cases, the men would be asked to change their behavior for women, as in this story from Susan:

I used to walk into backrooms of wholesale distributors, and needless to say, those are pretty raunchy. There might be calendars with photos of naked women on the wall, things like that, and I would just ignore them, until one day, Henry went in with me, and he looked at me to see if I was uncomfortable. He took the guy aside and asked him to take it down.

Colleen, who was raised in the 1950s by all those strong Southern women, attributes the end of her career to the phenomenon of the old boys' network. It was a painful ending after years of conflict with the male leadership team at Mercantile. She introduced us to Mercantile in part 1; here she shares more about the culture there and the struggle she endured in trying to perform a job for which she was sure she was capable:

When I left the ad agency environment to work for Mercantile, a corporation that had been in business for 20 years, I expected something completely different from what I found. If I had to describe the culture there, I would say it was a relaxed working atmosphere, no one wore ties. But it was relaxed to a fault. As Mercantile grew, and as I became more entrenched after working there so long, I saw that it was a company hesitant to change. They did not encourage new ideas or new thinking. The owners built their business without a lot of the constraints that major corporations have because they had no stockholders and didn't have to deal with all the laws related to that. As they grew, Mike Jr., who was president, didn't realize at first that because he now had hundreds of employees, he needed to have rules. They didn't have personnel policies. They made it up as they went along. Accounting was one bookkeeper who had been there for 20 years, who wrote things up in the books with a pen. That was in 1996. They were just starting to, being forced to, make the transition to being a big company.

I was very proud of Mike Jr., because he realized he needed to bring some people in, that they needed managers who could keep up with the growth. I was the first professional person they had hired since Tim, the CFO, was hired five years earlier. I was hired as director of advertising. He also brought in a director of marketing and a director of IT. And it wasn't all men. Besides me, the director of HR is a woman. The director of purchasing is a woman. The director of legal affairs is a woman.

The positions held by the other women at Mercantile are all in the type of support roles that are not career paths that lead to the top. The people that wielded power in this company were still all men, with Colleen continually struggling to be perceived as part of the power structure.

Here's what happened: the culture at Mercantile got stuck in the good old boys' club somehow. I don't know how that happened with so many capable males and females in the company. How does it happen that even the females consented to create this environment?

I have to wonder if they really "consented" or if they were just powerless, due to the level and type of positions they held. Colleen's culture story represents an example of a company that is, as she describes it, "stuck in the old boys' network." Colleen was surprised by this. She had a successful career up until her time at Mercantile and thought, as many people do, that the gender wars in the workplace were over.

Sharp, smart guys that I respected at the outset fell into the good old boys' club. I'll give you an example. There are seven or eight of these guys that go to lunch together every single day. It is the most ridiculous thing I've ever seen how they all run out the door and climb into these big old SUVs. Mike Jr., 30 minutes is all he wants to take for lunch, so you have to gobble your lunch down. It's sad; it's like something out of a cartoon. The guys feel that they have to go with him. What's interesting is that the other women, like the director of purchasing, director of legal, or HR, they were never invited. Only I was invited, the director of advertising, and I never quite understood that.

The men apparently understood that Colleen's position, unlike those of the other female directors, was a power position. Even though they had difficulty granting that power to Colleen, they knew to invite her to lunch!

I used to go, but it got so ridiculous. As the company grew, literally, there were nine of us going to lunch. It's silly. When you get in there the guys would embarrass the daylights out of me with their rude behavior. They are pulling tables together and yelling, "Get over here!" I was mortified. After a couple of those experiences, I told Mike Jr., "It's not that I don't enjoy your company at lunch, but everybody's talking loud. Everybody's eating fast. I don't enjoy it." He was very offended by that and I think that was a huge mark against me at some point. But it was a joke at Mercantile, "You going to lunch with the boys today?" That's what it was called: "Going to lunch with the boys."

Women continue to struggle to learn what behaviors are expected in the upper echelons and they are often put into awkward positions, like when the men go to strip clubs. Some advice books tell women to play along with these sorts of games, but when viewed from the outside they really do appear, as Colleen felt the boys' lunch was, ridiculous. In this case, Colleen's gen-teel Southern upbringing may have just been too offended by the behavior of the men at lunch, or there may be more to the story, but in the end, she knows that her choice to separate herself from the group at lunch was a strategic career mistake. Given the other women in the company and the way they were perceived, it may not have made a huge difference, but participating in lunch with the boss was one factor that she at least had some control over.

At one point I was actually told by Steve, when he was my boss, that he needed somebody that was better suited to work in the male environment of our retail stores. In other words, get down and dirty in that environment. He said that to my face. The stores were franchises and we only had two or three female storeowners in the whole 200 stores. The others are all white males, all of them. They have one female owner that they treat like she is from outer space. In fact, she was one of the ones that called me when the announcement was made that I was leaving. She asked me how I was doing, what was I going to do, and told me how much she would miss my contribution. She was the most professional of all. There is another lady who has owned a store for a dozen years. She is in the top ten stores and she's considered a rebel. She wrote me a card. She congratulated me and said, "What took you so long?" I think she's terrific. She's considered a rebel because she tells Mike Jr. what she thinks.

Colleen feels that the voices of women are devalued in this company, even when they are in the position of franchise owner. Colleen's voice, that of a seasoned professional in a field of exper-tise that was important to the businesses' growth and success, was also devalued:

Steve would always disagree with me. He made it clear early on, when he was director of marketing and I was director of advertising, that he was in one camp, and I was in another. When they promoted him to marketing vice president, he started throwing that weight around in a very big way. Over the next year and a half, I did my damnedest to try to deal with him. He was so cocky and such a big shot and would just say things in meetings that weren't correct. He would say he was going on a store visit and be out of the office for a week and nobody knew where he was. He was just all fluff and he was making twice my salary. It just got so bad that I quit.

I just walked into the Mike Jr.'s office and quit. I said, "I can't take this anymore." I was very polite about it, I said, "This is ridiculous, the man is beginning to usurp my authority here." I reminded him that I had been running advertising in the company all these years, and all of a sudden Steve has a title that gives him the ability to do a, b, and c.

Mike Jr., a conservative soft-spoken man, was flabbergasted and about had a heart attack. He did not see it coming. So here's the way that all came out: Mike Jr. and his dad convinced me to take a sabbatical. My mother had recently died of cancer; I was worn out. I'd been travelling back and forth to my home town. I think everything had just crashed down and I said, "There has got to be a better life than this." They gave me two months off, and promoted me to director of marketing and hired a new advertising director to work for me. They gave me some of Steve's responsibilities and said I would report to Mike Jr. in hope that some of the conflict would go away.

Well guess what happened? When I came back from the two months off, I was director of marketing but I was reporting to Steve, the VP I didn't get along with! From day one he did not want me in that position because I was not his handpicked child. Mike Jr. put me in that position to save me, so he says, but obviously it was just a snowball running downhill. I knew within a few months that between the CFO, Tim, who was now also an executive VP, and Steve, VP of marketing, there was no place, no voice for me at Mercantile. It was very, very sad.

I went in for my performance review with Steve about six months later. At that point in time I said to myself, "Okay, I'm not going to quit, I'm going in to stir it up and see what happens." Well, I did, and he fired me. He basically said, "I'm not firing you, I'll give you the ability to leave if you so choose, but this is not working out."

Despite all of her strength, not to mention her competence and tenure with the company, Colleen knew it was time to concede this fight. The interesting question to ask here is how a man in the same position, with the same successful track record and strong voice, would have been treated.

I think I intimidated Mike Jr. and Tim, the CFO, because never ever was I concerned about looking at both of them and saying, "No, I disagree with that and here's why." Disagreements between men happened all the

time; Mike Jr., Tim, and Steve disagreed all the time, but they man-
aged to work through it. I think also that Tim did not think I was worth
$120,000 year, no woman is. I made twice as much as any other woman
in the company and I just don't think he could deal with that. My head
was banging on that ceiling. He couldn't handle a woman at that level.
He thought if I was going to be at that level that I should have my own
building and be running a division. I thought, "Basically, that's what I'm
trying to do. If you could get Steve out of the way, I could handle this
myself."

I will not, I will not stoop to do what a lot of women are doing in that
company. They don't make waves. They just acquiesce to do their jobs and
don't believe that it would make any difference to speak up. I'm not certain
where that comes from. The other women at Mercantile are not going to
change it; they're not going to make any changes.

Colleen is actually pointing out that the other women in the
company were powerless, but she doesn't seem to realize it. She
doesn't understand why they don't "make waves," but she also
knows their salaries were half of hers. She seems almost naïve in
this. From other stories that she tells, it appears she does not want
to put herself in a separate class from her female colleagues, some
of whom were also friends. Aligning herself with them may have
worked against her. This decision supported the viewpoints held
by the men in power—that she was not one of them. The boys
have their club and she has chosen to join instead the less powerful alliance formed by the women in the company.

After I resigned, Mike Jr. wanted me to come and see him, an exit
interview. I said to him, "Quite frankly, I haven't formulated what it is I
want to say to you. If you would let me have some time, I will come and
see you before I leave." He agreed, but then, last Thursday, I went out to
lunch with Kim, a woman who works for Tim. She runs the accounting
department. We're sitting there having lunch, talking about life when in
walk "the boys." It was Mike Sr. and Mike Jr. with Tim, Steve, and
Bill, the director of IT. There were seven or eight of them. You should've
seen their faces! Mike Jr. just comes over and pats me on the shoulder and
keeps walking. Mike Sr. leans down and gives me the traditional kiss on
the cheek and says, "How are you?" I said, "Sir, I'm doing fine. Thank

you for asking." That's all I said. The other guys, it was like a movie, they were all bumping into each other and walking through the bar to get to a table in the back, so they wouldn't have to come by my table. These were the people I worked with all those years.

When I came back from lunch, Steve came in my office and said, "Mike Jr. and I decided that we think it's best for everyone that you leave now, because it seems that it's uncomfortable." I said, "Well, I'm not uncomfortable, but I know you guys are terribly uncomfortable." So he walks me downstairs; I turn in my laptop, key to the office, and I was gone. The thing that bothered me a lot about that company was they presented themselves as, "We care about our people, we're family." And then they treated me the way they did, after years of hard, hard service and dedication.

Colleen was saddened and is still bitter by the way she was treated. She feels a real loss for having to give up what she worked so hard to achieve, but she is realistic enough to realize that she could not change the environment. This is how Lost Leaders come to be—they eventually tire of the struggle to be heard, to be listened to, and to be respected as the competent business professionals that they are.

It was really hard the last few years. My soul had just been dying. It was dying. I could feel it. I would go in the office and feel like I was walking with a cloud over my head, because getting things done was tougher and tougher. It all fell apart when Tim was promoted from CFO to president, because he wanted absolute control and he did not support the direction I was taking. The thing about jobs is that the guys at the top, they know what they want you to do, and so, if you do that, everything is okay, but then you want to do something else and it's something they haven't thought about, I think it freaks them out.

It was an eye-opening experience, the way that ended. The good old boys had decided that they did not want a senior-level woman making decisions in that company. That was the bottom line for me: it was the good old boys club. I felt like I was set up. I could have been a real bitch and fought it, but that's not my nature. At the end of the day, I would still have been in that environment. I can't change it. Even if I had held on and held my position, I would have had to deal with that every day. It's not worth it. But I have my integrity. I have my accomplishments.

The "old boys' network" represents a subtle form of sexism that continues to pervade Corporate America. Even when individual players, male and female, are not acting in a sexist manner, the time-honored traditions are hard to overcome. One of those traditions is that women hold positions in support roles, not power roles. Colleen's role in advertising could be viewed as supportive, but the way that she embraced it, and her dedication to moving the company forward, caused it to be more powerful, or at least she wanted it to be. But the men who actually held the power were not ready for a woman in such an influential role. Women originally entered corporate workplaces as secretaries. The fact that they now hold positions as directors of human resources or legal services, as the other women at Mercantile did, can be seen as progress. That progress, however, is not enough for the women in this book who wanted to be leaders.

Colleen admits that not joining the "club" worked against her at Mercantile. As silly at it seems from the outside, being part of the group can affect an executive's climb up the ladder. Women are often counseled to try to be part of these clubs, but they sometimes do not feel they fit in. In the next chapter, the Lost Leaders will talk about their struggle to figure out the rules of the clubs. Patricia, who shared above that she did not want to give up her Saturdays to be in the club at Big Box, told of almost missing out on her dream job because of it. She was overlooked in the recruiting process; no one realized she had the skills:

An opportunity came up in a new department called "improvement systems." It was a small group of people that were handpicked to do process improvements. One of the five or six people that were in that department left to be a director of one of the business units, so there was an opening. I waited and waited for the job to be posted, but a posting didn't go out. I finally realized that they were just handpicking someone else. At that point it was all males in that department. I think a little while earlier they did let one woman into it, who had a very compliant personality. From what I heard, I pieced together that at that point they were just getting ready to ask this guy in IT to take the job. I knew they were going straight to the IT people, because that's who they went with before.

But I had passion for what they did, and I knew I'd be good at it, so I said, "What the heck." I'd been with the company four years at that point, and I was a good performer. I scheduled an appointment with the person who was hiring, the executive VP/CFO. I was pretty evasive about why. On the way into the meeting, I stopped at the office of my boss, the controller, and said, "Hey, I'm going to meet with the CFO and I'm just going to ask about that opening in improvement systems." And he said, "Okay," and then I scooted out. So I kind of went through the right channels. I reported to the controller, but this was the CFO's pet depart-ment and the CFO was the controller's boss.

I told the CFO that I knew someone had left and asked, "I assume you're going to fill the position." "Yeah." "I just have a question for you. What are you looking for in that position and would I have that skill set?" He's got this big bald head. He sat there doing this [motions rubbing his head] *and he said what he was looking for, and says, "Yeah. You do have the skills. I was thinking IT, but you do." Actually a lot of our account-ing staff had the exact skill set, analytical processing. So they stopped the hiring process. The CFO said, "I want to look at all of the accounting people." There was another round of interviews and I went through the process, and I got the job, much to the controller's chagrin. He felt jilted, and that's another story. He couldn't even talk to me for awhile. He's just one of those guys. He looked at it as a lack of loyalty or something.*

But I was just so excited I couldn't stand it. Honestly, I think the con-troller had a plan for me, and it was to be an assistant controller, but that wasn't what I wanted. So I went to improvement systems and I worked on all kinds of different initiatives for process improvements, but also on major new initiatives in the company.

Luckily for Patricia, she heard about the opening before it was too late. Although she is generally a rule follower and waited for the job to be posted, she was also savvy enough to realize when she had to take the initiative. The CFO at Big Box was also willing to have his original assumptions challenged. In chapter 9 there are stories of more blatant forms of discrimination where male decision makers were not willing to admit they had closed off opportunities to legitimate candidates.

Despite how unimportant, and sometimes how humorous "boys' clubs" might appear on the surface, they have a serious impact on opportunities for women at the top level of organizations. The Lost Leaders are painfully aware of this fact. The "old boys' network" is their term for the informal processes that favor a select group, in this case certain white men, over everyone else, particularly women. Since men and women often socialize in separate spheres outside of the workplace, this behavior is part of the taken-for-granted nature of the sex roles in our society. The fact that it is taken for granted makes it difficult to see this as a subtle form of discrimination. Although some women try to ignore the boys clubs, there is always an undercurrent of "who knows who" that impacts the climb up the corporate ladder and limits access to the power structure within an organization. Men are often apt to discount the discriminatory nature of this behavior, espousing equal opportunity, despite the fact that their closest confidants typically look just like them.

Here Pegge tells of being recruited for a position where the leadership tried to pretend that they considered women part of their club, but she saw through it:

EngineerInc sold my division. Because I had a lot of very key client relationships in growth areas, the buyer wanted to keep me, but the division headquarters was moving to a small town in the South. I wasn't sure if I wanted to move, so I went on a trip just to check it all out.

I knew pretty much on the first day that it wasn't for me. The company had one female executive, which was using the word loosely, and they paraded her in front of me about 12 times trying to accentuate how important she was. You could tell that she wasn't. It was a beautiful, beautiful little Southern town with big houses and front porches with rockers. I could have found a house there without a problem. The job would have been a promotion for me but I know if I had gone there my career would have stalled. I didn't think the culture was positive for females. It would've been a step-up, but it wouldn't have been a good long-term step. If I'm going to uproot myself, it's going to be for the right opportunity. So I took a voluntary layoff with a severance package.

Mary Anne, who has worked with many companies over her years as an organizational development consultant, confirmed that even in highly structured organizations, with systems designed to prevent favoritism, it happens:

The structure's just on the surface; it looks good. Does it work? Maybe. It does in some cases, but I think, ultimately, when we dig down deep and peel the onion to the very core, people are going to hire who they want to hire, especially at senior levels, which is where you can really make a difference. Even though there are formal processes, I think people get hired sort of based on who they know and how they know them—and who they want, regardless of the structure. I might be a little cynical, but I think that's what happens.

The old boys' network controls "who they know," which is critical both to being considered for potential promotions, as Patricia shared, and to having a voice in the company, part of Colleen's struggle at Mercantile. Nancy, who has obviously given this much thought, continues here to make the connection between being part of the club and having access to positions of power:

At CompSales, all the female senior vice presidents are now gone. If you look at the top leadership, the top 15 people, there are not any women anymore. They ought to be saying "I'm going to make sure that the next couple of hires are going to be women," because it's the right thing to do and it's the right thing for the face of the company. In my estimation, it's not that hard. There are a lot of very talented, capable women; if you tell yourself you are going to find them, you will find them. For this reason I think, personally, that affirmative action is still needed. It's not like it was 40 years ago. It's not like trying to find a woman with an MBA and 20 years of strong business experience isn't going to happen. There are tons of us who could sit in the seat of a president of a US corporation, tons of us. To have any impression that we're not out there is just silly. But there are places where the boys go and the girls don't, and I think that that continues to sort of build, so that when they are thinking about who they want to be their next-in-command, they think about the person they feel comfortable with and who they know, instead of saying, "I'm going to go out and find somebody who is going to break that stereotype."

Rosabeth Moss Kanter provided some insight into the tendency of men to hire and promote men in her 1977 book, *Men and Women of the Corporation*.[1] This tendency can be traced to the beginnings of industrialization in America and England when entrepreneurs (who were white men) were personally responsible for all of the decisions in their own companies. As their businesses grew, others were needed to fill management roles. Trust and loyalty were obviously key in such positions and the business owners attempted to maintain control by only hiring from their closest circle of peers, often members of their own family. Although professional managers from outside the founder's family are now the norm, trust continues to be a primary concern in all hiring decisions, and the need for trust grows as positions get closer to the top of the organization. This leads the predominantly white male executives of today to hire people they know, people who they believe will make the same decisions they would. Those people most often also look like them. Clearly, the "old boys' network" contributes significantly to the creation and preservation of the "glass ceiling." As Nancy says:

What they do is they go in their own little network. This guy tells you about that guy who tells you about that guy, and it's all guys.

CHAPTER SEVEN

The Acceptable Band

In the mid-1980s, the term "glass ceiling" began to be used to describe what was happening to career women—they could see the next level of the company, but couldn't get there. With the 1987 publication of the book, *Breaking the Glass Ceiling: Can Women Reach the Top of America's Largest Corporations?*, the term became a permanent part of the discussion of women in business.[1] The book explains the glass ceiling as "not simply a barrier for an individual, based on the person's inability to handle a higher-level job. Rather, the glass ceiling applies to women as a group who are kept from advancing higher *because they are women.*"[2]

Supposedly written to help women, the book told us that the key to our success was to stay within a "narrow band of acceptable behavior." We were told that we, as the women of the moment, had to dispel the belief that women could not be leaders, while not forfeiting "all traces of femininity," something we were told would make us "too alien" to our male bosses. The book included a graphic of two overlapping "hoops" of behavior types, with a very narrow "acceptable band" of behaviors that fall in both hoops. The hoops are labeled "masculine or like men" and "feminine or unique to women."[3] The authors hint at how difficult it would be to even know what behaviors fall in the overlapped band, much less to stay within them—they then proceed to state that doing so is the most important thing that women can do to be successful in business.

At the time, the authors of *Breaking the Glass Ceiling* admitted that leadership and femininity were considered contradictory behaviors. Nonetheless, in 1987 and to a great extent today, women are told to "take risks, but be consistently outstanding; be tough, but don't be macho; be ambitious, but don't expect equal treatment; and take responsibility, but follow others' advice."[4]

This observation by Nancy was made while she was describing a woman who had been a vice president at Comp Sales, several years before Nancy herself reached the executive level:

I think there was a time when part of what women needed to do—right, wrong, or otherwise—to grow the idea of women in the workplace was to sort of get rid of their woman-ness, you know. And there was a time when women had to dress more like men, they had to tough things out like men do . . . they had to do all these things like men did, so that they would kind of fly below the radar screen.

This is an excellent depiction of the women of my own era, those of us who entered the workforce in the late seventies, when we were very often the only female in a meeting or on a management team. In addition to *Breaking the Glass Ceiling*, books like *The Woman's Dress for Success Book* and *Games Mother Never Taught You: Corporate Gamesmanship for Women* came out around that time with advice on how we could assimilate as much as possible into a world that was created by and for men.[5]

Other women gave these examples of their workplace atmospheres that valued what are considered masculine traits:

Patricia, speaking of Big Box: *The culture was similar to the military. It was very command and control. The top four people in operations, the vice presidents, were all similar, they were either really tall or had a booming voice.*

Joyce, speaking of Insight: *So my boss, somewhere along the line, chose as the mascot for our division a rhino, to use for awards. They give you a bronze rhino. It was all this "don't tell me you have obstacles in your way. You are a rhino, you blast through it." It was very macho, very male.*

When women try to assimilate to this leadership image, there is an ill-defined line they cannot cross. Being too much like the men, operating outside of the acceptable band, is "too alien" and not allowed. Mary Anne, who has been an executive coach for several years, made this observation:

I have coached women who have tried to conform to the male-dominated culture and the male-dominated leadership style and it's gotten them in trouble. They have tried to be too much like the men in terms of how they dress, how they act, and it has gotten them in trouble. They have been labeled as bitchy. They have been labeled as ineffective. They have been labeled as inflexible. They have seen what has been successful for the men; they have seen what has gotten promotions. They have seen the "heroes," so to speak, and they have tried to emulate them—and it comes off wrong. It does more damage than good to them in their careers.

The best example of a behavior that was read differently when seen in a woman is aggressiveness, a trait that is rewarded in men in the workplace but can be threatening when seen in a woman, as Nancy confirmed:

I firmly believe the men at Comp Sales could not accept aggressive behavior in women the same way that they expected it, in fact, in themselves and in men. People look at you like you are a bitch; you are not supposed to be that way. Aggressive with a woman is sort of a dirty word, while aggressive with a man isn't really. It's bizarre. It's fascinating. And it used to frustrate the shit out of me.

I mean all of the male executives, these men can be the biggest assholes, you know mean, you know horribly aggressive just mean, horrible, yelling people. The women at Comp Sales could be half that, we weren't mean in the way that we deal with things, we didn't yell, but we were aggressive and assertive when we had to be. We would be viewed negatively and told we were not getting along with our peers or whatever. And yet that exact same behavior from a male counterpart was viewed totally differently. Or maybe it wasn't viewed differently but they didn't feel the need to coach them or comment and say, "Oh this is bad," with the males, but they did with the females.

When I asked Nancy where she felt this leaves women in the workplace who want to succeed, she responded: "*I think that most successful women, albeit sad in a way, have to be able to tone down their aggressiveness, and still be really good at what they do.*" This, from a former senior vice president in 2005, is the same advice offered by the authors of *Breaking the Glass Ceiling* in 1987.

Susan spoke about the culture in her first corporate job at Mainstream Manufacturing, a company dominated by men. She was continually trying to determine what behavior was appropriate:

Mainstream Manufacturing was in the Fortune *100. They were a "number one in the market" kind of company and so, of course, everything you did was dictated, maybe not actually dictated, there wasn't a rule that said how you do something, but there was a penalty for not doing it that way. For example, in the old days we had plat bags. They were these big black, heavy, leather sales cases. They didn't realize that one of those was too heavy for a woman to carry, let alone maneuver into a car the way they prescribed a plat bag was supposed to be maneuvered into a car. So I went out and got a different case. I was written up for it because, in their eyes, their way was the only way that generated revenue. Appearance was also very important; you had to watch your weight. I was told I wouldn't be promoted if I didn't present a certain image [pauses].*

Here's a point I haven't talked about out loud. There was a culture; it was clear there was a culture. But there were no systems, no supports in place to teach women the culture. You just stumbled through and people laughed at you. If you stumbled more than once or twice, you were not part of the culture, and therefore probably were not going to be there for long.

I remember going to my first managers' meeting, when I was first pro-moted into management. I was one of four new regional people and we were asked to attend a meeting of more senior people. The senior people had already been meeting, and we were supposed to join them at a certain time of the day. Even the way we entered the room was dictated. I just entered the room, looked around, kind of read the room, and proceeded on. Later I was told by Henry, my boss at the time, that I didn't enter the room properly. "Well, how was I supposed to enter the room?" "Well, you should have just known." The irony of it was, that the person who should have briefed me, if there was in fact a protocol, was Henry, the very person that was criticizing me for not getting it right. I had an expectation that I would have been coached.

I remember thinking, back in my very naïve days in that company, "All I have to do is perform and they will take care of me for the rest of my life." Well, you've got to get over that real quick. The cost of them taking care of me was counter to my own set of values: the image thing, the weight issue. Even for the men at Mainstream there were certain physical requirements: no one with a beard, no one with a mustache.

Although this sort of image requirement was common for sales people at the time, and to some extend still is today, it represents a latent form of discrimination that impacted women more than men as the standards were less clear. I asked Susan if the "weight issue," which she mentioned more than once, was something that was applied to men also. She hesitated in her response. This is clearly something that is still painful for her. Finally, she said: *"I don't know that it did [pauses]. I don't know that it did."*

The behavior that was acceptable for men was very different. I can remember stories about some real old-timers who had to have their bosses go to the hotels where they were on the road, because they had gone into a drunken stupor. I'm sorry, but I would have been out on my you-know-what.

I remember the very first road trip I took with my boss, when I was first promoted into management. He had booked us into a lower-end kind of hotel. I said, "I ain't doing that." So we made a deal that we would stay at such and such hotel, if we went for a nice dinner together. So he took that as an opportunity to have a nice dinner with me, then go back to the hotel bar and have a nightcap. At one point, he said, "I need to go make a phone call." He got up and left me sitting at the bar and, as he left, he slapped his room key down on the table. He thought I would follow him, but I didn't take the bait. I just sat there and waited for him to come back from his phone call. There was certainly behavior that was acceptable for the guys that wasn't acceptable for the women.

In contrast to the struggle by women to find the behaviors for success, Susan gave an example in which the roles were reversed, where a man found himself in a stereotypically female situation and was unable to determine what behavior was appropriate:

The first sales staff member at Mainstream that ever got pregnant worked for me, and I remember saying, "Hey, we're going to have a sales meeting at the Four Seasons, let's have a baby shower." As it happens, the VP for sales came in for the meeting. He was politically correct enough not to be upset that I had done this, but he did not know how to act. He honestly was, literally, out of his element, so much so that somebody thrust a teddy bear in his arms to hand to her, and it was like, he could not do it, could not do it.

Picturing this hapless male may be humorous, but it is doubtful that his inability to behave properly at a baby shower limited his career success in any way. The contrast between this and a situation in which a woman is not sure of the appropriate behavior helps to illuminate the power differences between men and women in the workplace. We tend to laugh at the befuddled man in an awkward situation with women, but cringe at the woman who does not know how to act in a room of powerful men.

When I asked Susan if she felt her upward mobility was limited at this company, she quickly answered:

Absolutely. Absolutely. At Mainstream there were always conversations, every three to six months, about here is the path, here are the opportunities, here's what you have to do. It was a clear road. Not that there were no obstacles, but there was a plan. In my last position, after a period of time, after I'd created revenues, I said, "What's the plan?" Henry responded, "Well, we'll talk about that." I think the ceiling was in that job. When I raised the question again, he looked at me and he said, "You will not go anywhere until I say you'll go somewhere. It will be my choice."

Susan had much to say about this particular supervisor and the damage he did to her career. She later found out that Henry had been identified as the "consummate chauvinist" of the company. She was assigned to work for him as a test, to expose his bad behavior. Henry was not the only challenge Susan faced at Mainstream; she shares more stories from this time in later chapters. Despite having such a struggle at Mainstream, she had much success in her career. But these many years later, she still expresses the hurt from what she endured as a young woman in this male-dominated environment.

Mary Anne also struggled with appropriate behavior, although she was working in a less masculine, yet still very conservative business. Her personal style was not what was considered appropriate to an executive, which led to rumors about her true path to success:

In my own career, early on, it was 1990 I think, I proposed to the president of a large organization that he promote me to his senior management team in an advisory capacity for organization development. I was young and brave, I wore trendy suits; I was growing and I had no fear. I was in a financial organization, a banking and insurance company, so it was very traditional. There were only a few women on the team and there was a rumor that I was sleeping with the boss and that's why I got the promotion. For a woman to have gotten to the senior level, conventional wisdom was that she must be sleeping with the boss. I heard the talk, but I continued to just demonstrate my commitment; I was there to do the job. I was very motivated to do my job in spite of it. In time everyone could see what I was capable of, my level of education and intelligence. And so the talk died down. I ignored it. I didn't fuel it. I did my job and I was still brazen, outspoken, but I would think about appearances.

That organization had a lot of after-hours get-togethers and I was selective about going to those because of the rumors, walking the line of being friendly but professional, particularly with my boss. I was bound and determined to silence that rumor mill. You know, as a woman, you have to be smart and you have to be prepared for those kinds of things when you are out on the fringe and doing something that is different. I think you have to just expect sometimes that people will say things about you that are not true and you have to overcome it by continuing to show your commitment to the job. You're professional and you're capable of doing what you're doing because of your education and background and not because of anything else.

Mary Anne's description of this situation is rather matter-of-fact, as if this is all just part of the process—women have to prove themselves in ways that men are not asked to. At the same time, her tone is very defensive.

There were two other women on that senior management team: a chief marketing officer, who was married with children, and a woman from customer service who was in the process of a divorce with three kids. Neither of them was a very trendy woman, they were very traditional, and they were older than me. I was single at the time, no children, and had just gone through a divorce. I was the target of the rumors. But I didn't let it stop me, and I proved it wrong. I was just very mindful. I had to be selective, but I think that's just smart.

Although it may well have been smart to avoid the after-hours get-togethers, as it might be smart for women to avoid other situations in which the rules are so unclear, it does not change the fact that relationships are being built, "boys' clubs" are being formed, and, right or wrong, these impact everyone's career potential.

Mary Anne refers to her "trendy suits" as an issue for how she was perceived. Given that the fashion industry has never given up on the buying power of working women, many of us struggled to find the appropriate attire to emulate the men, without being too much like them. The men all seemed to know what they were supposed to wear to work, but we had no idea. I started out with dresses and some pantsuits but always felt somehow under-dressed when surrounding by men in grey and navy blue business suits with ties. Their lives just seemed simpler. I felt that I had enough to worry about in the competitive environment of public accounting, without stressing over what to wear. When I discovered John T. Molloy's *Women's Dress for Success Book*, published in 1977,[6] I was actually grateful. Molloy, who had already written the best-selling *Dress for Success* for men, told me what was best, and I just trusted him.

Molloy said that women who wore skirted suits with blouses were most likely to be perceived as successful, powerful, and "in-charge." The idea, it seemed, was to desexualize ourselves as much as possible, without dressing exactly like the men. So, our suits were also to be grey and navy blue and our shirts were to be conservative, even man-like was okay there, but we had to wear skirts, not slacks. We couldn't look like we want to *be* men—that is outside of the acceptable band, the kind of thing that makes the men uncomfortable. Given this had become the standard by the time of Mary Anne's story in 1990, we can only imagine what "brazen" and "trendy" choice she made. A coworker of mine was once reprimanded for wearing a skirted suit to work, because the suit was red.

Following Molloy's advice, we wore skirts. During that era, wearing skirts meant we had to wear pantyhose, something men did not have to deal with. In the winter that was probably a good thing, but summers in the South and pantyhose made very little sense. Joyce told a story about Top Tier, which was in a northern city with very cold winters. One day in the mid-1990s, she decided that it was crazy to wear a skirt and the requisite pantyhose and pumps. She was so "brazen" as to wear a pantsuit to the office. Within a couple of weeks, the majority of her female peers were also wearing pantsuits. Sometimes being brazen just made more sense.

My male colleagues, when defending themselves from our complaints that they did not have to wear pantyhose, would counter with how uncomfortable neckties were, in any weather. Men's neckties were a very important part of professional dress, but if women wore them we would cross into that unacceptable area again, the "imitation man," that makes the men uncomfortable. So someone, I would really love to know who, came up with what we all now affectionately refer to as "floppy ties." These were made of material similar to men's ties, but they were shorter and flouncy, not straight. A feminine version, if you will, of men's ties. I also don't know who came up with shoulder pads. In hindsight, this looks like an obvious attempt to look more like the men, to try to actually be physically bigger.

My favorite image of this time is the actress Diane Keaton in the movie *Baby Boom* (figure 7.1). She was wearing a suit (skirted, of course) that is cinched at the waist with a belt to emphasize the size of the shoulder pads, and one of those floppy ties. She is holding the baby that she "inherited" in what is, of course, a completely unacceptable situation set up by this movie to remind us that we can't have babies if we want to be business executives.

Figure 7.1   Baby Boom Poster.

The masculine environment also manifests itself in language, particularly in the use of profanity. Although considered acceptable in most of the environments the Lost Leaders described, they generally did not participate in it themselves. They did not feel it would be perceived as appropriate for them to do so and they were raised to think it was unacceptable behavior for "young ladies." The women didn't complain when the men used profanity, though; in fact, they generally chose to ignore it. More than one of the women felt that the fact that they did not allow cursing to bother them was a plus in their careers, as seen in these examples:

Susan: *There were also some situations where the language was rough. If it makes people uncomfortable, then it's improper, but some people can't communicate without it. So if you want to communicate, you're going to have to make it okay for them. I can't say that that was a problem for me. I considered it a compliment when another woman says to a guy at the table, Susan's okay* [laughing], *meaning they could curse in my presence.*

Barbara: [Laughs]. *You will get a "Pardon my French." I never ever took things as I'm a woman, therefore, I will take it a certain way. I don't.*

The presence of women in formerly all-male business meetings may have thrown off the men who were used to being able to use rough language there. They had been taught not to use such language in front of women, creating a dilemma. It is debatable whether this challenge gave women some sort of edge, or whether it caused the men to feel resentful that the women were even there.

But what about the acceptable band? Can women join in when the language gets "colorful?" In the 1989 Supreme Court case *Hopkins v Price Waterhouse*, the men evaluating Ms. Hopkins' potential for partnership in their firm were concerned with her behavior, including her being "a lady using foul language."[7] Nancy is the only Lost Leader here who admitted that she participated in this practice, feeling that she had to conform to the confrontational style of her boss, but she admits *"that's a style that I turn to as a reaction, it's a style that I use when it's necessary, I'm confronted with it."* She provides the most dramatic example of this in the story of an interaction that she had with Comp Sales' president. She will share it in chapter 10.

My father had what he called "selective hearing." He heard what he chose to hear. He also had a saying, "The good Lord gave me two ears, one to send and one to receive." I know it makes no sense, but somehow we knew it meant that we could ignore things that were said if we chose to, like he did. I was able to put this advice to work when I was in environments that were predominantly male. The men I worked with did not seem to feel they had to "watch their language" when women were in a meeting. Instead, I noticed they would talk quieter when they were saying something that they thought I might find offensive, so I just pretended I didn't hear. Like Susan and Barbara, I didn't think objecting to the use of off-color language was useful to my career success.

The confirmation hearing of Clarence Thomas was a watershed event for women in the workplace. The senators may have chosen to ignore Anita Hill's testimony, but the coverage was so intense that it sparked many, many conversations about what is and is not appropriate behavior in the workplace. For some it may have been the first time they ever really understood that sexual harassment is defined by what makes the harassed person uncomfortable, not what the harasser considers crossing the line. I remember a male coworker and friend coming into my office during that time. He was quite sheepish when he asked me if he had ever said or done anything that I would consider inappropriate. Now, the men I worked with at that company were pretty much inappropriate all day long. This was an environment in which I really had to test my selective hearing. I was getting older, more secure in my career, and my patience with the fraternity atmosphere was wearing a little thin. I can't remember what I told him, I know I let him down easily, but I do believe my answer was that yes, he sometimes said things that were inappropriate. But I told him I had never been terribly bothered by anything he had done, because I was "used to it," or something like that. I hope that his newfound awareness benefited the women he worked with in the future.

I don't really understand why men need profanity and off-color humor to communicate, but I have seen plenty of examples of it, and they always think it is hilarious. Most women just chalked it up to "boys will be boys." But, thanks to Anita Hill, we had reason to believe that we could object when it crossed a line that we got to draw.

Separate from the off-color language issue, other word usage is notable in the stories here. The women do not want to be labeled "bitch" or "bitchy," but do not comment on the fact that these words apply only to women. Terms like "aggressive" and "heroic" are used for the men, often for the same "bitchy" behaviors. The women also said they did not want to be, or could not be "girly girls" or "little girls," terms typically used to describe negative behaviors of men who are not acting manly enough. I find it interesting that the childish behavior of the old "boys" has a very positive, powerful connotation, while being a "girl" is automatically considered a negative.

After language, the issue of drinking was the most-often discussed behavior the women struggled with. Barbara, who says she never let the "old boy" nature of business stand in her way, told some of the most outrageous stories about drinking, and was clearly fed up with having to be a witness to such behavior. She spent most of her career at BGV, a large organization in a regulated industry. It was a professional environment and an affirmative action employer. She was given many opportunities for advancement, but turned some of them down to limit her travel and avoid transfers, both of which conflicted with her family responsibilities. When her division was sold, Barbara was hopeful for an even brighter future. Instead, the environment changed dramatically, and she eventually lost respect for the company's leaders. Her stories of the new company's culture are somewhat amazing, even though drinking and cursing were the norm in many of the work environments described in this book.

When my division of BGV was sold and the new company took over, the culture followed the leader, and that culture was one of a total lack of respect for people—the CEO yelling at people and saying, "Who do I fire for this big f-up?" There was drinking and carrying on. I'm not a teetotaler, but certain things are appropriate in certain places. The culture that the company took on was one that I wanted to leave. I don't know if that culture's prevalent in many corporations, but it is in this one.

The last international trip I took, I was with three vice presidents. These were people I really liked personally, but I just lost so much respect for them. They were drinking and partying and it was like fraternity days. I just can't drink like I did in college because I get sick, you know. Here I was, away from my family, we are there for a business purpose; we need to close this deal, a huge negotiation. They are just talking about how they were drinking all night on the overnight flight. I met them in the afternoon. We had dinner, talked about what we needed to do the next day. I went back to my room, while the three of them went out to the bars. They were out till three, four o'clock in the morning. They had no sleep.

The next day, we managed to get through what we needed to get through with the client, then we went to lunch without the client and these guys were just laughing about it all, just like a fraternity, "We drank so much and weren't we funny." And I'm thinking, "I'm in another country with you guys, and I really want to be home with my family." Then, at the airport, we were at the executive lounge and they can't wait to start drinking again. We get on the plane and they are drinking and they are laughing and they are loud. Two of them just have loud voices. So finally, a passenger in front got up and yelled an obscenity at them and all of a sudden they're like, "Why are you getting so mad?" And I'm looking at them, trying to pretend I don't know them, as this fight is breaking out. One of them, who is an attorney, all of a sudden switched and turned his attorney hat on and said, "We're sorry, but you don't have to get obscene. You could have just asked us to be quiet."

They were all VPs of BGV and they got in on the buyout and they own part of the new company. Now that it was no longer part of a big organization, the culture allowed that kind of behavior. It was now more accepted; you would not get in trouble for it. I hear it has gotten worse since I left. People will say to me, "Barbara, you look so great," because I'm happy. They tell me: "It's worse. It's worse than ever." I will talk to people and they are saying, "I've got three more years; I'm just hiding out here."

How can it get worse? Let me just give you an example. At the big annual customer conference, every one of the vice presidents was so drunk. One of the customers is a nudist. She is not into anything sexual, she just feels comfortable in her body. So after a night of drinking, she strips and goes into the pool and is skinny-dipping. One of the vice presidents drops his drawers and gets in with her. Now, you want to talk about corporate culture? What are the employees saying? "Now I know I can't do any-thing too wrong. If he didn't get fired, there isn't anything I can do at this company that is going to get me fired." Everybody knew about it. How could he not get fired? Because they condoned drinking, and because his boss, who was there watching, was too drunk to say anything.

I had an employee who, when she was traveling, would drink to the point of being drunk, where people would have to help her back to her room. When she drank she would sometimes say something inappropriate in front of a customer. I reprimanded her for it, and she couldn't believe that I did it. She said to me, "Well, everybody else does it."

Barbara is clearly exasperated by what she sees as cultural issues. She doesn't see it as a male versus female problem, but Mary Anne, Nancy, and Susan all feel that women are held to a different standard. We have to ask if this behavior is appropriate in any business environment and what this says about the leadership and productivity of American businesses, not to mention our popular culture and the prominence of alcohol consumption. Can a woman, a Mormon, or a recovering alcoholic, succeed if they do not participate in this behavior? There were many stories of after-hours drinking, and women often struggle with how they fit in what Barbara so aptly describes as a fraternity-party atmosphere.

This incident was a catalyst to put Barbara on what she calls her "faith-based journey" to find a new career. *"My whole thing is just respect. I have no respect for them,"* she told me. She does not feel that they discriminated against her, but they put her in a position that was clearly in conflict with her values. Despite this, she makes excuses for finding the behavior objectionable, telling me that she is not a "teetotaler," she just can't drink like she did in college. She mentioned this three times, almost seeming to question if she should have tried harder to fit in. She does not address what might have happened if she had attempted to keep up with the male executives and their "fraternity" behavior. She also never suggests that she should have complained about it. She likely did not feel either of those choices was available to her.

Certainly there are men that would not accept this type of behavior as reasonable in their businesses, but in Barbara's company it was acceptable. The executives in the airplane and swimming pool stories were leading a business that had recently been purchased from BGV, where they held similar positions. BGV had a very structured environment with well-developed policies to protect it. Any lessons these male leaders might have learned there do not seem to have carried over once they were outside of the control of that structure. But then again, maybe they did learn something at BGV. Barbara also said:

It was not that it wasn't there in BGV also. They would throw big customer parties and there was always a lot of drinking and carousing. Our meetings were a great excuse for these men from Podunk, Iowa, to go on a business trip and have a big fun time.

Other Lost Leaders alluded to the use of alcohol, both during business travel and office functions, including routine happy hours after work. Stories of sexual harassment (although not labeled as such by the women) were often tied to situations where alcohol was involved. Drinking is clearly a part of the culture of these businesses and an area that is difficult for women to navigate. If they act too much like men, they open themselves up to allegations of being unladylike, but if they are not tolerant of this behavior, they are considered prudes (another female-only term) or too inflexible.

"Acceptable band" issues of appropriate male and female behavior are particularly difficult to address in the workplace, because those roles transcend the business world and are ingrained in our culture. The traditional role of women as "caretakers" follows them into the corporate boardroom and conflicts with the expectations for leaders that are found there. Men, on the other hand, can maintain their "provider" roles both in their family responsibilities and their work as leaders of corporations. These norms for the behavior of women and men must be addressed before "equal" treatment of women and men will achieve equal results.[8]

The research organization Catalyst conducted studies of the glass ceiling in 1996 and again in 2003. They surveyed CEOs and female executives of multinational companies. Over half of the females identified male stereotyping and preconceptions of women as significant barriers to their advancement in 1996. By 2003 this result was reduced, but one-third of the women still expressed this concern. In neither survey did the male CEOs recognize this as an obstacle.[9]

The same study asked about behaviors recommended for women trying to break through the glass ceiling. Developing a style with which male managers are comfortable was suggested by 61 percent in 1996 and 47 percent in 2003.[10] The barriers identified and the behaviors suggested show a continued focus on the women and what they can do to succeed. Like the many books of advice available during my career, the focus seems always on what women can do, trying to "fix the women." But when we are truthful about the acceptable band, we find that there is no behavior that is clearly acceptable. The band is just too elusive. Until women are allowed to be themselves and still be seen as leaders, many will be lost. The price is just too high, as Nancy shares here:

I remember when I was in public accounting. It would have been 1985 which wasn't that early, but there were only two women partners and this was in a very large office with 1500 professionals. One of the women partners was in tax and people would say, "Oh, she's in tax," like that is some sort of different, not as great thing. The other one was just your classic old-time woman professional. She dressed very, very conservatively; she had children, yet she worked like a dog, a million hours, gave up her life, basically, to sort of prove something. She was the classic woman of that day. I remember thinking to myself, and I wasn't even interested in children back then, didn't think I ever would be, but I remember thinking to myself, "If I have to give up who I am, I don't even care, it's not worth it." But thank god for those women, those women certainly were the ones who laid the groundwork.

CHAPTER EIGHT

The Ideal Worker

In her book, *Unbending Gender,* law professor Joan Williams describes the workplace as having been built around "ideal workers" who are available continuously and full-time—because they have no responsibility for housework or childcare.[1] For the executive-level positions held by the Lost Leaders, the ideal worker is expected to be available to work long hours and be able to travel and relocate. Williams argues that this constitutes discrimination against women, since they are also expected to take primary responsibility for childcare and other needs of maintaining a home for their families. The women's movement of the 1960s and 1970s demanded equal access to jobs, but stopped short of addressing the fact that, once we got the jobs, we had to deal with these competing expectations. Even when they did not have families to care for, women are often viewed as less than "ideal," due to the cultural norms that expect women to eventually assume domestic duties. Williams believes that men are also suffering from the requirements of being ideal workers, and that both men and women find it difficult to succeed without conforming to this standard. Here is how Williams describes the alternatives available to women under this system:

> They can perform as ideal workers without the flow of family work and other privileges male ideal workers enjoy [because they have wives]. This is not equality. Or they can

take dead-end mommy-track jobs or "women's work." That is not equality either. A system that allows only these two alternatives is one that discriminates against women.[2]

At the time *Unbending Gender* was published, 90 percent of top male managers had nonworking spouses, demonstrating how pervasive this family structure is at the level of the corporate leader.[3]

Husbands sometimes take on the primary responsibility for childcare and housekeeping, while their wives establish careers. In these cases, it is the men who have become Lost Leaders, so that the women can be ideal workers. Although this may be seen as an improvement from the prior generation, when choices for women were more restrictive, it is not a solution to the problem of losing leaders. The fact that we refer to the men who take on day-to-day responsibility for the family as "Mr. Moms" reinforces the idea that what they are doing is *supposed* to be done by women.

In addition to working long hours, ideal workers are often expected to be away from home overnight. Business travel was the primary reason that several of the women here became Lost Leaders. Travel was even more of a challenge if they had children. Pegge and Barbara told these very heartfelt stories about their children, who played a big part in their reasons to give up jobs that required travel.

Pegge: *I had to take some time off, had to have some surgery, not a big deal but I was off work for a little while. One day my husband was out of town and I had picked the kids up at car line—I didn't know what car line was, it's long!* [laughs] *So I'm in car line and I get the kids home and we get all their homework done, and we have this really healthy dinner, because I actually cooked, and we had all this playtime. So we got out the Lincoln Logs and we are in the living room and we've got Lincoln Log forts everywhere, and we've got cowboys and Indians and we are just having a ball, and it suddenly hit me like a ton of bricks: I am missing way too much and I need to change my life starting tonight.*

Barbara: *I had taken a weeklong trip out of the country; it was the first week of December and was supposed to be my last of the year. The next week I had to leave again, a last minute trip, and I missed something at my daughter's school. I was on the phone with her like I am every night when I travel. She was in tears and I'm trying to tell her, "I'll be home tomorrow," always trying to be real upbeat, positive, "I miss you a lot, but this is important for Mom, and I'll be home tomorrow." I asked her what she had for homework, and she said, "I had to write a letter to Santa Claus. You want to know what I asked for?" It was for Mom not to have to take any more trips. That was like [cringes]. So I came back from that, took two weeks off at Christmas for vacation, and when I went back to work, I knew it was temporary.*

It was not only women with children who felt that they were missing something in their lives. Mary Anne was seeking better balance:

I was diagnosed with a health issue last fall, a very rare and difficult sinus problem. It's a sinus that is the farthest back in our head and very near our carotid artery, our optic nerve, and our brain. My doctor suggested a pretty risky surgery. I had also gained a lot of weight since my divorce. I was running around, traveling around so much and I hadn't been exercising. Now with this serious health issue and the surgery, I really stopped, took a look around, and said, "I am unbalanced in my health, for one area, and there are a multitude of other interests," just some other things that are really meaningful to me, and I'm not making any time for any of this. And so that drove me to want to get in control of my schedule. I'm really in a work–life balanced time in my life again which is important to me, and it had nothing to do with kids.

The jobs Pegge, Barbara, and Mary Anne held included a requirement to travel and, for the most part, they did not begrudge their employers for this demand. Some of the Lost Leaders expressed hope that technology could reduce the need for travel in the future. As more companies become national and international, however, it seems likely that many jobs will continue to require travel, which will be a challenge for women, and men, who want to have balance in their lives and time with their children.

Long work days while in town also present a challenge to working parents. Nancy expressed the hope that at some point women who choose to work shorter hours in order to be with family would at least be viewed the same as men who work shorter hours:

I think as people get more comfortable with working around people different from them, and realizing that although this awesome executive leaves by 5:30 every day because she wants to be home with her kids, that doesn't make her less professional, or less capable, or whatever. You might have in the workplace a male executive who leaves at 5:30 because he's some particular orthodox faith who has to be in some church thing. They never think that person is less capable. They think he puts in fewer hours, but they don't think he's less capable. Today they look at the woman who makes a family-type choice as less capable.

Nancy recognizes that when the choice is to be with their children, women have been devalued. Note that her comparable male example is not leaving for reasons related to his children. This is especially interesting, since Nancy's is married to a "stay-at-home husband."

Workplace flexibility and work–life balance are terms that have come to be associated with retaining women. Because policies intended to provide balance have been tied to women, and specifically to women's roles in childcare, they seem to have done as much damage as good. Executive women who want to be viewed as serious about their careers and not have their prospects limited have shied away from taking advantage of these policies, even when they are offered openly by their employers. Nancy provided an example of the backlash for using one such policy, the Family Medical Leave Act (FMLA), by a younger woman in her company, who she feels is extremely well qualified but was held back, subtly, early in her career:

There was a time early on where they had an attitude about her; a really, incredibly sexist, stupid thing. Her first child was born with a birth defect. Her baby had open heart surgery at like two weeks old and she stayed out. That was just when family medical leave [FMLA] came out, and she stayed out the whole 12 weeks [allowed by the law], and they had an attitude about it. How stupid is that? And she was only a manager then. They had an attitude about "she took so much time off." That's arcane, but true; it was pretty bizarre.

FMLA is available to men and women alike, but attempts to make this and similar policies apply equally have mostly failed in the corporate environment. I believe this reflects a concern by men that they would be viewed as less committed if they avail themselves of such policies. If workplaces become more accepting of male executives who put a priority on their family responsibilities, it will be easier for both men and women to achieve the goal of balance.

The requirements on the ideal worker are reinforced by legislation, such as the Fair Labor Standards Act of 1938 (FLSA), which created the 40-hour workweek and overtime pay. Although the purpose of FLSA was to prevent employers from requiring employees to work excessive hours without appropriate compensation, management and executive positions are exempt from it. Today over one-fourth of the workforce is exempt. Because they are "exempt" from overtime pay for hours beyond 40 in a week, managers and professionals have come to be seen as "owned" by their employers 24 hours a day. Although the criteria for exemption were revised in 2004, the discussion surrounding the rule changes did not include any indication that this basic presumption of the rule is suspect: that "exempt" workers, due to their managerial status, are not forced, or even coerced, to work excessive hours. Executives today are expected to work long hours and are rewarded for being seen in the office in the evening or on the weekend. The advent of technology that allows them to be "connected" 24 hours a day has only worsened these demands. This seems to be against the spirit of the original FLSA, which was enacted because Congress found that there were "labor conditions detrimental to the maintenance of the minimum standard of living necessary for health, efficiency, and general well-being of workers." Although I recognize the importance of these laws in protecting workers who are in powerless positions, it seems to me that managers and executives, and many others classified as "exempt," have had their "standards of living" compromised by the demands of the workplace also.

This is how Patricia experienced this phenomenon at Big Box, which led her to join the Lost Leaders:

It was a face time culture and face time in a town 50 miles from my house. With kids, that didn't work for me anymore. Luckily, my earlier bosses at Big Box had been pretty open-minded. They knew I was a single mom for five years with little, little kids. I was living closer then. They knew that I would do whatever I had to do to get the job done. And they were sort of, "Okay, work the hours you need to work." But there were people there who just couldn't stand that I would come in at nine some days and some days leave at four. It was kind of a military culture, very face time, but more than half the time that managers are there after hours or on Saturdays, they're bullshitting. It's just face time. Unfortunately, that helps in that environment, you know, you are part of the club. I never did that. If I had to go in on a Saturday, because I had to get something done, or because I wanted to leave the next week on Friday at noon, I got in and got it done and went home. I know that I would have had a more... [hesitates] but I still think I did well.

A system in which men work long hours, while equally capable women limit their careers to take care of the home and children, seems innately inefficient for businesses. The Lost Leaders are not contributing, and the men (and women) who stay in their careers are working excessive hours, reducing their effectiveness and eventually burning out. This has also resulted in businesses being led by the leaders who are the most available, not by those who are the most competent. As Joyce observed:

I never felt like the senior people at Top Tier were the best and the brightest. It was a great place to learn, but I felt like the people who moved up were the people who towed the line and sort of stuck it out. They weren't people that dazzled me, I can tell you that much.

Business leaders are being selected—not from all the potential candidates, but from only those who are willing to work the hours, to be the ideal workers. Often, these leaders, men and women alike, feel they "paid their dues" by working the hours and they are less likely to work to change the system so that others do not have to do the same. Joyce shared two examples of executives who blatantly stated that they were not supportive of attempts to change the culture, at least not in how it related to the treatment of executives. The first case was at Top Tier, a company that had an active program for what is called "workplace diversity":

I remember when a general manager said to my boss, "You know, I don't think work–life balance works at the director level." I mean, he literally came out and said that. I just thought it was interesting that a general manager would come out and say, overtly, "I don't think this works at the director level." Like if you want to be successful, higher up the chain, that doesn't work anymore, that's for the people at more entry levels.

Joyce's second example was from a company executive that she interviewed when doing research for a book:

One of the senior guys basically said, "Yeah, I'm not sure I really believe in the whole work–life thing; I'm not sure I believe that it's our responsibility. That's the employee's problem."

Joyce's book is on the topic of work–life balance, an issue directly related to the concept of the ideal worker. These executives are saying that they do not think that the requirements of the ideal worker need to change, especially when someone reaches a certain level in the organization. Unfortunately, this attitude has been shown to impact women disproportionately, due to societal expectations that they take primary responsibility for caregiving and maintaining the home.

Some men who are living up to the expectations of the ideal worker also struggle with their choices, as Mary Anne saw with a coaching client of hers:

He is behind the bleachers at his kid's soccer game on his cell phone. His wife has told him, "I'm about done with this." I'm coaching him and he said, "You've got to help me get control of this. I know this is out of control, and I know that this is not a good example I'm setting on the inside of my company or for my marriage and my family." But then, he said that, "I am so passionate about what I do, it's such a huge part of who I am, I can't stop it." And I said, "Aren't you a father? And aren't you a husband?" Then he really, he got tears in his eyes. And he said, "I almost feel like I don't know how to turn it off," and he said, "Honestly, I don't want to." He loves it. He loves it and I think a lot of men who are successful, at the top, feel that way. They work those hours because they love it so much. They're passionate and it is so a part of who they are, they're almost not able to see why it isn't that way for everybody else. They really struggle understanding that. And if someone says to them: "I have a family," they say: "So do I. Why can't you give more? Why aren't you more committed?"

This presents an interesting example of the way that the ideal worker role has impacted men. Although he thoroughly enjoys his work, this man also wants to do the right thing for his family. Given the business culture that he faces, he cannot see any way to be successful without working the long hours, sacrificing his family time. But he is in a position to change this culture, isn't he? In a competitive business environment, one executive, even at the very top of a company, feels powerless to change it. If his competitors don't do the same, he thinks he will lose business, and he is probably right. Until the overall culture changes, it is difficult for individual players to make the change.

Mary Anne also knew women who stayed inside corporations and complied with the ideal worker requirements who, she says, are happy with that decision:

I've worked with women all over the country and there are many that are part of organizations in corporate America that I don't think would have it any other way, women at the top—director, VP, executive VP level. I don't at all think they would have it any other way. They really enjoy what they do. If you interviewed them, you would find that a lot of them are the breadwinner of the family. Their husbands may work, may not work. Many of them don't even have children. They are not traditional families. It's a very nontraditional family; the woman is usually more successful or higher up than her husband.

Although these women may very well be happy with their life choices, the fact that they are often childless or have husbands who don't work is additional evidence of the resiliency of the demands on the ideal worker. For these women to be ideal workers, they either gave up having children or their spouses gave up having careers, because ideal workers with children need the support of "wives." It's as simple as that. The amazing thing is that Mary Anne did not acknowledge this at all. She was using the fact that these women enjoy their jobs to be supportive of the corporate environment to show that women can succeed. Mary Anne makes this argument in spite of the fact that she herself became a Lost Leader in order to live a more balanced life.

Patricia chose to leave a successful career in public accounting specifically because she wanted to have a family:

I left the accounting firm because I was married and we were going to want to have a family. No female at the firm before me had a child. I did not want to be a guinea pig. I decided that I would tell the managing partner that that's why I was leaving and tell him that if he didn't get a program in place for working moms he would lose more. They didn't want to lose me because I was doing well. There were a couple of women that I knew there who wanted to start families. He was pretty receptive and they actually did get something going and had some degree of success. I was glad to see that. I didn't put it in writing or anything, but that was why I left.

Patricia didn't abandon her career at this point; she went to work at Big Box, a company that held itself out as family oriented. Unfortunately, the culture there eventually changed, and she was left to try to adapt her life to fit it. In this story, she tells of two attempts she made to change the new culture at Big Box, which required long work hours. An interesting twist here is the presence of a female leader who pressured the professional staff to work those long hours. That woman was older than Patricia and, like the older women in this book, did not have children. Early pioneers as female executives often sacrificed family for career, but Patricia's peers were trying to find a way to "have it all." This female executive fit the profile of someone who, having paid her dues, expected the same of those who followed her:

When I joined Big Box, the accounting department was small, probably less than 20 on the professional staff. It was fairly family oriented. We had a nice culture. Every month we had birthday celebrations. We would all go in the coffee shop and literally sing to whoever was having a birthday that month. You started work between eight and eight thirty in the morning and you left at five. I took a little bit of a pay cut to go to work there out of public accounting, but I didn't have all the travel. I didn't have to work all the hours; no one at my level was working Saturdays or Sundays. The leadership, though, the treasurer and controller, worked Saturdays. They always came in every Saturday, along with the CFO, for three hours in the morning. It started with the treasurer; when she was hired she started working Saturdays. She was the controller's peer, so he started working Saturdays. Then the CFO started coming in Saturdays.

In the early 1990s, the economy wasn't doing great and the company really had to tighten its belt, so the treasurer and controller started to require that their staff members keep these little manual time sheets. They were handwritten at first, later they went on Excel, but we just literally put in what time we came in and what time we left, subtracted lunchtimes, whether it was a half an hour or an hour and a half. If we left for doctors' appointments or if we left early on a Friday, we had to subtract that. We were required to show that we had worked 45 hours a week, net of any time away from the office. It was amazing how, once I started having children, and started having issues with them being sick and taking them to routine doctors' appointments, there's all this time you have to make up. So I was using my vacation time to keep the numbers right. I went for a year or two without a vacation and then I went through a divorce. Go figure.

What Patricia does not acknowledge, and perhaps still doesn't realize, is that this practice is borderline illegal under the Fair Labor Standards Act (FLSA), which created the 40-hour work week (discussed above.) Since these employees are considered exempt under FLSA they should not be required to track their time. They are being treated like nonexempt, hourly paid workers. If they are actually being "docked" for working less than 40 hours a week, it follows that they should also be paid overtime for working more than 40 hours a week. They are being required here to show 45 hours and, as Patricia shares below, being applauded for working even more than 45. The "exemption" does not seem to be working too well for them, does it?

Here is the rest of Patricia's story:

Later, after I went to work for the controller, managing one of his departments, I tried to raise the issue of the time sheets. There was this morale survey that would come out annually. At the end, there was an open comments section. I'm so idealistic; I thought they wanted to use this to improve things. So I wrote something in and I trusted the process, which was supposed to be confidential. I wrote: "I'm fairly okay. I'm somewhat overqualified for the position that I'm in, but I feel this job is the right thing for me to do for the company right now." But I also wrote: "These time sheets have got to go. We are professionals." I basically gave my two cents about the time sheets, in an anonymous fashion. A few months later, when the results were tabulated and shared with management, the controller called me in his office. He figured out, because I was somewhat overqualified for my position, that I wrote the statement about the time sheets.

The reason I lasted there as long as I did is that I believe the controller means well. In this case, he wanted to make me feel better, so he said to me, "Patricia, you are my top performer. You are my top dog, don't worry about the time sheets, but look at this." Then he pulled out a spreadsheet. All of our time sheets are going into a spreadsheet and are listed in order by number of hours worked, quarterly, and annually, and I am at the bottom of the list. He says, "But I hold you as number one." I responded, "I'm an overachiever. I don't want to be at the bottom of any of your lists; it crushes me. It crushes me, even though you're saying it doesn't matter." They also had quarterly meetings, where they pat people on the back, whose average is 60, 65, and 70 hours a week, which tells everyone that more is better.

I had an infant at that time and I knew I was going to have a second child. I said, "I literally cannot be at the top of that list in the next five or ten years, because I can't balance all of that and be what I need to be as a mother." I wanted to ask him, "Why are you even keeping this spreadsheet, if it doesn't matter? And why are you patting people on the back once a quarter for working more hours?" Can I tell you what he was thinking? "If only I could get her to work 10 or 15 more hours!" He did recognize that I could achieve more in 45 hours than other people were achieving in 70, "But what if I could get her to work 70?"

This executive, Patricia's boss at the time, and the treasurer of Big Box, who together instigated the use of the timesheets, both came from public accounting. Professional staff members in those firms are required to keep timesheets for the purposes of billing clients. Although policies vary between firms, the one I worked for considered staff below the manager level nonexempt and paid them overtime. That the leaders at Big Box felt they could make the same demands without a comparable compensation system is troubling. It should be noted, at the time this occurred, Big Box, a large regional company had no human resources or personnel department to advise them on such matters. As Patricia will share in chapter 9, they have since faced two large class-action lawsuits for employment discrimination and have a very busy HR department today. Here, she tells of the second attempt she made to change the culture there:

About two years later, when I was head of my own department, I decided to take a major morale killer and turn it into a positive. If we have to track hours, then why can't we work different kinds of hours? I had the approval of my boss and the company president. They still wanted 45 hours net, so it truly equates to a gross 50- or 55-hour week, a little bit unmanageable. I talked to my boss about letting me work from home, to do things I can do on Saturday morning, when my kids are sleeping. That way I can be picking them up at six o'clock every night when daycare closes. I told my boss to look at my department's productivity, because we measured it. Look at our morale. It was the highest in the company. Look at the turnover. It was nonexistent. That's why my boss left me alone. He was hands off. His philosophy was that each department gets to do their own thing; they do what works for them and their style. The controller and treasurer wanted us to run our departments all the same way, because nobody wanted to go to work for them. If I had to keep the hours they wanted, I would have quit five years before I did. My boss, he was open-minded enough to allow the flexible schedules. He couldn't care less, as long as you're getting the job done.

Patricia eventually left this company, becoming one of the Lost Leaders. This issue of work hours was part of the reason for her decision to leave. Her boss and mentor at Big Box left first. He was the only one there who supported her in working the flexible hours that made it possible for her to do her job and spend the time she wanted to with her family. Here she reflects on her relationship with him and the impact of his departure and, later, hers:

Along the way, I expended a lot of my political capital to support him. I was told he would always protect me, and then he was gone. If he was still there I would probably still be there. I would probably be a vice president.

All of that flexibility of work schedules went out the window when I left. The controller and treasurer were not open-minded about work hours. The controller had a wife and a nanny and the treasurer had no children and a husband that is retired. You can't apply that lifestyle. Do you want people who don't have families? Can we not procreate? What's the deal? They claim to be a family-oriented company, but they don't want your spouse to work. Two of the three women who were promoted to vice president, their husbands stopped working before they were promoted. The third is not married. That is what the treasurer would push them to do. The treasurer was female, but we come from different places. I can't fit her mold (working long hours) and she doesn't get my mold (flexible work hours.) She thinks that I'm not being a professional because I prioritize my kids.

Patricia is obviously happy with her choice to prioritize her family, but she knows that it impacted her career advancement. The fact that women at this company are actually told they need nonworking spouses or no children in order to move up is revealing. It demonstrates that the culture of business, built around men with stay-at-home spouses, is resilient. Women can share in the power of running companies, but they must do so within this model.

Joyce worked in companies where women had moved up and she saw how conforming to the ideal worker model had impacted their families:

I saw friends of mine at Top Tier having children and it seemed like such a raw deal for everyone. It seemed like a raw deal for the kids. It seemed like a raw deal for the moms. Despite the fact that Top Tier is featured in the Wall Street Journal *at least once or twice a year for being a great company for women. Women get promoted to very high positions. So they say, "Well, see? A woman can do it." One of the key leaders at Top*

Tier is female and she got written up in the Wall Street Journal *a couple of times. I knew her. I don't want this to sound mean. She's a mom in her own way, I guess, but she wasn't a role model for me. Her nanny raised her children. That's her choice and that's fine, but to me, that was not the role model of what I wanted to do for my family. So that certainly was in the background of my decision to leave corporate. I couldn't figure out how I could even add children into this equation. I'm in the office at seven in the morning, which means I'm out of my house by 6, 6:30, at least. I'm never home before seven, many times more like nine. So how do you add kids to that? We wanted to have kids, we knew we wanted to have them at some point, I just couldn't see how you did it.*

The ideal worker ideology impacts all women, not just those who are married or who have children. The ideology is based on a stereotype of workers with no responsibility for day-to-day life activities, which is an expectation that is difficult for single men and women to fulfill, as Susan shares in this humorous anecdote from her time at Mainstream Manufacturing:

None of their wives worked. I would even challenge my bosses when they would say, "You know, you'll fly in on Sunday night, on Monday we need you so-and-so." I'd go, "When am I going to do laundry?" They would look at me like I had three heads, "Laundry? Never thought about that." I pointed out one day that every one of them had a wife who packed his suitcase, did the laundry, and so they miraculously have the suitcase. The practicalities of life were something that the men, never, ever understood. And it wasn't like I was a prima donna about it. I'm not a prima donna [laughs].

Even when women are willing to give up "work–life balance," whatever that might mean to them, and behave as ideal workers, they are often stopped by the "glass ceiling." Those with power over their careers make assumptions about their capabilities and commitments, by virtue of their being women. This results in discrimination against women, when their superiors act on the perception that women *will* marry and have children *someday*, and either quit working or lower their commitment to their jobs. In an example of Nancy will share in the next chapter, even when she had no intention of reducing her commitment after having a baby, her managers did not consider her a candidate for promotion, based on their own preconceived notions of the behavior of women with children.

Susan, who did not have children, had another interesting experience at Mainstream Manufacturing, where there was a company philosophy that favored men with families:

Up until the time they hired me, they hired only men with either a fiancé or a wife, with plans to have children. They were very honest. They said, "This is our strategy. We want people to have a reason to have to stay." Well, they looked at me, and they said, "Shoot. Now what do we do with her?" They couldn't find the albatross. I had let it be known that I wanted to buy my first house. The day that I was promoted, I was called into the regional office. I was told that I was being promoted with one condition. They said, "You buy a house this afternoon." They knew I was very close to finding one and that was the albatross, the reason to keep me working, if I had a mortgage. I couldn't have a family or kids, god knows. They couldn't figure out how that would work. But if I had a mortgage, that could be the albatross to hold me.

This old-line established company knew they needed to hire and promote women and they acknowledged that Susan was producing on par with the men in her sales position. At the same time, they could not let go of the management philosophies that worked when all their employees were husbands who needed to support a family. Instead of changing the philosophy, they would try to figure out how to make it encompass Susan. Here is how she sums up her tenure with Mainstream:

There were pluses and minuses in their strategy. For the longest time I said, "Hey, I'll play the game. I'll get the pluses out of this whole situation. I've got to work anyway." But it was a game. As I look back, I knew it was a game. The insulting part, and that's the first time I've ever used the word insulting, the degrading nature of that, what eventually causes you to walk in and say, "This is it," is they didn't think of it as a game. They didn't figure out that I did. It was almost like they thought their employees were too stupid to figure out their game. "We'll only let people through the bottleneck who we can trust with our game." That's just me editorializing.

Pegge also worked in male-dominated businesses, and her employers, EngineerInc and Consolidated Manufacturing, continually offered her many opportunities for advancement. These companies were government contractors subject to affirmative action laws, and they were happy to have a female engineer on their payroll. Working for such companies was a boon to a talented professional woman like Pegge. The opportunities they offered her, however, required relocation and travel, choices that were difficult to balance with her husband's career and their parenting responsibilities. Pegge's story represents the dilemma faced by two-career couples:

Consolidated was very interested in promoting me up within the ranks, but in the meantime my husband was moving up in the ranks within his company and eventually he was president. That really limited what I could do. One other important point is that we wanted to have kids, but I was still in the position where I was traveling all over the place. When a sales position came up, I took it. A lot of people viewed it as taking a step back. I actually got a lot of advice not to do it, but it's a life choice. If we were ever going to have kids I couldn't be traveling like that. So when the position opened up, I took it. Did I love it? Sales is fun, so I had a lot of fun with it. I had a little, small territory, so I could come home every night. Hence we had two kids.

The company continued wanting me to take different positions. There were a lot of opportunities, but I couldn't move. I would tell them, "Hey, thanks, good, appreciate you thinking of me, but my life is here, I can't." So there was nowhere to go. Then my responsibilities increased and the travel, even in my sales job, became more frequent, and my husband's business travel was picking up, and we were juggling the kids, and I was thinking, "I can't keep this up anymore." You know in your life circle, your physical, your mental, your social, at the end of the day, all that was really suffering was me. I wasn't taking any time for myself. I wasn't sleeping. I was dreading work and I knew that I couldn't keep doing that forever.

At the end of the day, I absolutely loved what I did in business and was exceptional at it. The company was trying to continue to provide challenges and new things, but they knew that they couldn't give me the next level promotion because I couldn't move. All that being said, it was just strictly a life choice [to limit my career], *that's all it was. It's just a life choice decision, and a good one.*

Pegge's "life choice" is one that many women struggle with, as do more and more men. She doesn't question these demands from her employers; she accepts travel and relocation as reasonable requirements for career success in business. In a workplace built around men with stay-at-home spouses, this made at least some sense. Although it put burdens on the stay-at-home mothers, at least traditional families could find ways to cope with this demand. We can speculate, however, that excessive travel and multiple relocations take a toll on families.

Pegge continues to deny she faced discrimination during her career; she did not experience any overt acts of discrimination and, in fact, was offered many opportunities to advance. I would argue that the structure of the workplace that requires travel and relocation represents a type of discrimination, but Pegge clearly does not see it that way. Neither women nor men should have to make such tough choices between work and family priorities. There must be another way to structure jobs. If American businesses want to stop losing leaders, both men and women, who put their families as a priority, this model will need to be challenged.

As long as the price for success continues to include being an ideal worker, men and women who stay to take on leadership roles will be making a sacrifice that the Lost Leaders here did not wish to make. I believe that everyone should have the opportunity to have a complete life of her/his choosing, not just those who can find a spouse who will donate his/her career potential to cover the domestic duties, so that the business leader can give all of her/his efforts to a corporation. Patricia shared this sad observation:

Two of the most powerful male vice presidents at Big Box, I don't know why they decided to tell me this, they were 50 to 55 years old and both told me, "I worked my kids' whole childhood away. Now I want to spend time with my kids, and they're basically saying 'f- you.'" Their kids want nothing to do with them. They recognized I wasn't doing that.

Yet by not doing so, she became a Lost Leader.

CHAPTER NINE

Against the Law

In this chapter, the Lost Leaders tell stories of more blatant forms of discrimination. In some cases the women protested to corporate leadership, but none of them filed lawsuits or joined in class actions. Only in the past few years have we seen women professionals involved in employment litigation to any great extent. In the early years, we truly felt we were lucky just to be allowed a chance to participate in the male-dominated business world. We were willing to look the other way when such "slights" as overt discrimination were occurring.

The stories in this chapter are more factual, more straightforward than those in other chapters, where instances of discrimination are more subtle or covert. The issues here would appear on the surface to be easier to address; a law exists, it should be followed. The fact that blatant discrimination persists is evidence of the taken-for-granted system of sex roles which overcomes the logic of the law. This is at least part of the reason why we have yet to achieve true equity in the workplace, and why I believe that affirmative action is still needed.

Employment discrimination is prohibited by Title VII of the Civil Rights Act of 1964. The primary goal of Title VII was to prohibit discrimination against blacks; an opponent of the legislation added the word "sex" in an attempt to defeat it.[1] The first director of the Equal Employment Opportunity Commission (EEOC) has been quoted as saying that the sex provision of the

Act was "a fluke...conceived out of wedlock."[2] *The New York Times* dubbed it the "bunny law," referring to the dilemma of whether a man could sue the Playboy Club if he was not hired to be a bunny.[3]

In addition to this obvious bias against Title VII, the EEOC was initially given very little power to enforce it, and its authors were careful not to mandate any sort of preferential treatment, instead focusing on eliminating barriers (e.g., Jim Crow laws). This concession, and the absence of enforcement power, is what ended a 534-hour Senate filibuster against the Act, allowing it to pass.[4] The administration of President Lyndon Johnson favored a much stronger policy, and it came eventually in the form of Executive Order 11246, which created affirmative action. Issued in 1965, this order required government contractors to submit plans that "analyzed the demographics of their existing workforce and indicated proactive measures the employer would take to move toward greater equality."[5] The Equal Employment Opportunity Act of 1972 gave the EEOC power to initiate complaints and sue employers, and extended its jurisdiction to include groups other than racial minorities.[6] The Pregnancy Discrimination Act of 1978, an extension of Title VII, protects women by requiring that employers treat pregnancy like any other disability.

In a 1986 case, the EEOC was able to establish that the Sears Roebuck Company had exhibited a pattern of discrimination in favor of men for high-paying commission sales positions while women were concentrated in lower-paid jobs. Sears presented a defense based on surveys of applicants that showed women "lacked interest in the commission sales positions because they were competitive, high pressure, and had irregular hours."[7] A federal court of appeals upheld this defense, known as the "choice" strategy and it is still in use.[8]

An important case for women executives was decided in 1989. The international CPA firm Price Waterhouse had denied partnership to Ann Hopkins, despite her successful record of performance. Her personnel file included criticism of her dress and demeanor, with her superiors noting that she was too macho, aggressive, "a lady using foul language," and needed to take a "course at charm school." Hopkins was counseled to "talk more femininely, dress more femininely, wear makeup, have her hair styled, and wear jewelry."[9] The Supreme Court, for the first time, considered this sex stereotyping to be a form of discrimination under Title VII.

Also in 1989, the federal agency that enforces affirmative action, added "corporate management reviews," also known as glass ceiling reviews, to its audit program. Government contractors could now be held accountable not only for their hiring practices, but also for retention and promotion of women and minorities.[10]

Unfortunately, affirmative action has been used in such a way that many now consider it a code word for reverse discrimination, the lowering of standards, and the use of quotas.[11] It was not until the passage of the Civil Rights Act of 1991, which allowed punitive damages, that employment discrimination lawsuits became attractive to private attorneys. The large settlements in the headlines over the past few years are a result of this change in policy.

In 2001, the EEOC filed a class-action lawsuit against Morgan Stanley, then one of the largest brokerage firms on Wall Street, claiming that there was a system in place that precluded women from gaining access to the most lucrative accounts and created a hostile environment where such activities as trips to strip clubs were the norm.[12] The firm stepped in before the trial date and settled this case for $54 million, although they denied wrongdoing.[13] Despite this experience, the firm found itself the subject of another lawsuit in 2006, this time by a woman who alleged that her sexual harassment complaints led to retaliation by the firm that included overlooking her for promotions and taking away important accounts.

Boeing settled a class-action lawsuit related to discrimination in pay rates and promotion of women workers for $72.5 million in 2004, the same year that a sex discrimination case against Walmart was certified as a federal class action. That suit was the largest class action in history and the potential damages to Walmart were estimated at $2 to $4 billion.[14] The Supreme Court ultimately threw out the Walmart case, saying that the individual situations were not similar enough to constitute a single class. The lawyers have not given up; they now plan to file class actions in individual states. In October 2011, they filed suits against Walmart stores in California, and in January 2012, against those in Texas.[15] In October 2012, a similar class action was filed in Tennessee covering stores in that state as well as parts of Alabama, Arkansas, Georgia, and Mississippi.[16]

Nancy, Patricia, and Joyce experienced blatant forms discrimination, which they will share here. Not only did Nancy and Patricia uncover biased treatment, the male managers responsible were so bold as to admit to it. Nancy was told explicitly that she was not considered for a promotion because she had just had a baby. This specific bias has been labeled "the maternal wall":

When Comp Sales was looking for a controller, I had been there for several years in the director role and I was clearly the best director they had; I was clearly a viable candidate. But even though in a lot of other cases they did plenty of promote-from-within things, they were really jerking me around for quite a while, in terms of whether they were taking me seriously as a candidate. They were parading in people with my exact background, but men—people who looked like a bright shiny penny, like a résumé looks. So I decided to update my résumé and I actually sat down with my boss and said, "Look, I'm just as capable on paper, as all these people, plus, you know me, I have the skills." My boss, a man probably five years younger than I was, most of them were young, he said to me, "Well, you know, we're not really sure," because I had had a baby. "We're not really sure if, because of your family situation, you'd be able to make the commitment we're looking for."

Now, my husband was the stay-at-home dad, had been forever. I had never missed a day of work. When I had my baby I was out exactly the six weeks [of short-term disability] *and oh, by the way, still keeping up with messages, conference calls, having meetings, and everything else during the whole time. There was absolutely no reason, nothing, to even justify their concern about my commitment. I ended up writing a letter to the CFO and the manager, attaching my résumé. It said, "First, here's why I think I'm a great candidate." I made the letter as positive as possible, but* also said, "I feel it's important to respond to your concern about my family situation." I reminded them that I'd not missed a day of work, not gone home early, that my husband was the primary caregiver. I pulled a lot of the cards that men pull, you know, "I'm the primary provider, I need to provide for my family."

Patricia, who was also the breadwinner in her family at the time, found out that she had been paid less than a male with the same credentials, and the manager responsible had done it intentionally:

There is a guy who started at Big Box after me and they brought him in at a higher salary. And I know from my boss that she questioned the controller about it, because this other guy who came around the same time, went to work for another department, with the exact same background as me, and the controller's response to her was, "He's got a mortgage to pay." I mean, I was married to a blue collar worker. He was making $15,000 a year. I had a mortgage to pay!

In both of these incidences of overt discrimination, the Lost Leaders' male supervisors based their decisions on stereotypical sex roles. Women are not expected to be the breadwinners and are not expected to commit as much to their careers, particularly if they have children. What makes it even more interesting, and frustrating, is that both of these women *were* the primary providers in their households. In addition, Nancy's husband was staying home, in the caretaker role. These factors apparently were not sufficient to overcome the stereotypes held by the decision makers in these companies.

Although she was not a party to it, Patricia's company settled a class-action lawsuit regarding promotion of women. She worked on the team that developed a new career path to correct the situation:

The class-action lawsuit was only in one department, where women were not having success becoming managers. A group of about ten of us worked for a long time on this; we reorganized the structure within that department. We put in a structure that had all these different established departments and career paths. Ninety-five percent of the department's managers didn't want to do this, because it was so different. It was not *the way they came up. They came up being what was commonly called "second man," and you had to do manual labor in that job, you literally had to be able to do heavy lifting.*

This class-action lawsuit received a great deal of media attention, which I believe was primarily because of the popular belief that women have equal opportunity. Patricia's description of this situation shows that the discrimination was at least partly built into the structure of the jobs. Entry-level positions that women traditionally held never led to management; while those for which men were recruited, jobs that required no more experience or education, had a direct path upward.

Another example of the maternal wall was shared in the previous section. A younger woman in Nancy's company was held back subtly because she took a full 12 weeks of FMLA after her baby was born with a heart defect. This woman may never have identified a specific act of overt discrimination, but Nancy, an executive several levels above her in the organization, was aware that the men in power used this instance as proof of reduced commitment to the job. The fact that this woman's baby had a serious medical condition, and that she only took time that is available to her by law, causes them to look particularly heartless, but does not stop them from perpetuating the stereotype. The Center for WorkLife Law in California has publicized cases where women were routinely assigned less important work after returning from maternity leave. One notable quote in their work is from an attorney who was given work that could be done by a paralegal when she returned from leave. She said that she wanted to tell them, "Look, I had a baby not a lobotomy."[17]

Joyce also identified an incident at Top Tier that she felt was sex discrimination, and was willing to point it out to the company leadership:

Top Tier was so conservative, by the time you got promoted, you were so capable of doing the next job that you were bored. That was always a little frustrating. It was too slow. Mark, the director I worked for in marketing, was also my informal mentor. We had a great relationship. When I transferred from finance to marketing, he said, "We are moving

*you over and you will be on a fast track with a promotion in six months."
I cruised along, everything was great, my six month review came up and
my manager, who reported to Mark, said, "You are doing great, everything is fabulous and you are set to get promoted in a year." I didn't
even bother having the conversation with her, because she didn't have the
authority. I went to Mark and said, "We had this agreement." He said,
"I know, but things are changing in the company and now it is not a matter of when you will get promoted but if. You are still completely on track,
you are doing great, but we can't do it." So I sucked it up like a good
soldier and said, "Okay."*

*Within a couple of weeks, I happened to be at a company function
and one of my coworkers let me know that a male counterpart, who
moved from finance into marketing at the same time I did, got promoted.
Now, he did not have an undergrad in marketing and he was not going
to business school at the time, which was supposed to be required to be in
marketing there. I was almost stunned. There was smoke coming out of
my ears!*

*The next day we were offsite at a sales meeting and I left a voicemail,
in no uncertain terms, for Mark that said, "You will make time for me
today, you will." So he did [laughs]. I laid it out just exactly like this:
"This guy moved at the same time as me. He does not have an undergrad
in marketing, which I do. He is not in business school, which I am. We
moved at the same time and we were basically told the same thing." I said
"I know it shouldn't be sex discrimination, but it sure as hell looks like it."
He said, "Give me a day." I was promoted within the day.*

*He blamed human resources. He said, "I was told one thing and I was
playing by the rules. The other guy wasn't. It's HR's responsibility to
keep track of this sort of thing. They didn't catch it. You are promoted,
you get this raise." The bummer part of it was that I deserved the promotion. I was already doing the job. It takes all the joy out of it, to get it that
way. I also knew that the guy who got promoted was not viewed as being
particularly exceptional or gifted among our peers.*

Although Joyce's example may well have been due to lack of
oversight by human resources, she felt that she was being treated
differently because she was female. Perhaps the manager of the
male employee who was promoted was more willing to bend the

rules for a male, or perhaps the male employee was not as willing to accept the lack of promised promotion. Regardless of what motivates the behavior, in many cases the result is the same—the women lose out. Both Judy and Nancy pointed out that after downsizings at their employers, MegaBank and CompSales, both major corporations, very few women remained in the executive ranks. Judy's feels that MegaBank particularly targeted executive females and employees over 50, two categories that she fit:

I think what happened is that Corporate America, in my mind, from what I've just seen in the last few years [as an executive recruiter], *and looking at it in MegaBank, had the opportunity, through the auspices of downsizing, to do their rightsizing in who they wanted from who they didn't want, and the percentage of people they didn't want were older, and were predominantly, in my industry, female.*

A few women survived the culture change, but some of those women were viewed as pets or had personal relationships with some of the men. They are not viewed as people who did it on their own. That's a tough thing to say but I'm going to have the courage to say it.

Up to the point of the downsizings Judy refers to, MegaBank had a long history of providing opportunities for women and minorities, and well-established affirmative action and diversity programs. Judy believes that they used "downsizing" to reverse those years of progress, reflecting the underlying bias that still existed among the top managers. The company had undergone two significant mergers, so these top managers may have come from other institutions, but this experience left Judy bitter about the true state of "equal opportunity" in the United States. This bitterness can be seen in many of the stories she told and was clear from the tone of voice she used when discussing her departure from this company in Part 1, although five years had passed. As a former regional vice president of human resources for one of the largest corporations in the country, Judy also had some strong opinions on the topics of affirmative action and what she terms "latent" discrimination:

There are people that know what they have to do, and especially what I consider to be high-level managers. They understand the law. They know what the company stance is, but they have a personal agenda and a personal mantra that is diabolically different, and it shows, from the way they promote, from the way that they give out their increases, the way they stand up and praise someone, to their inclusion, in the sports activities that they pick—how they eliminate the female. Employment laws are very nice and good, but I think people are very smart today. They can avoid blatant discrimination, but there is something else that I consider to be latent discrimination, and they absolutely, positively, know how far they can go. They sabotage women's success, or they aren't really open to having females participate in certain things. We have affirmative action, we have laws in this country, and companies are not even held accountable. Lawyers get them out of it. Big business has the money to get umpteen different lawyers and, even when they are guilty, they still get away with it. That's despicable. There have been some large settlements, obviously, someone got sloppy. But in relationship to the amount of discrimination that goes on, it's miniscule.

Nancy, who overcame the "maternal wall" and went on to become a senior vice president at CompSales, a *Fortune* 100 company, has this viewpoint about the glass ceiling:

I think that the world sort of kids itself. Or at least this country kids itself, when they think there's no glass ceiling. It's just higher than it used to be. It used to be that women were allowed to be good secretaries, nurses, and teachers, and [now] women are allowed to be good managers, and good middle managers, middle-level executives, but you still don't see women respected as much as they should be, more in some sort of gender-neutral fashion, in my mind, in the board rooms or at the highest levels. Just like you see, we're not ready for a female president [of the United States], apparently. It's the same thing as people can deal with women in Congress, because there are so many of them. If you get one woman, that doesn't take one of your two spots. But then there are far fewer senators, from a percentage standpoint, and president and vice president have never been touched.

Were you to ask them, my guess is the vast majority of people would not respond like that advertising guy who said that women are stupid. People would answer with all perfectly wonderful things about how capable women are and they can do everything men can do. It would be unusual to even get a glimpse of people's real inner prejudice, because I'm not even sure they recognize it in themselves.

Nancy is referring to a 2005 incident in which an executive at one of the largest advertising agencies in New York, responding to a question about why women were not seen at the top in that industry, said it was because "they're crap."[18] The former president of Catalyst, who is now a professor at the Stern School of Business, when asked her reaction to this man's comment replied: "He spoke out loud what all too many men in leadership positions believe but don't articulate...They act on those unspoken biases, and it becomes a self-fulfilling prophesy."[19] Nancy continued her argument:

I bet if you asked the average CEO, especially the younger ones, "If you had two candidates for your company president and one was male and one was female, which one would you hire?" I don't think they'd immediately say the male. They would say, "It depends on the qualifications." If you said, "Would you be open to the woman as much as the man?" they'd say, "Yes." I think they truly believe that they've done everything right, but the numbers don't prove it out. If they were doing everything right, there would be more women at senior levels.

As to why things haven't changed, Mary Anne, who has worked with many companies in her consulting practice, feels that the top managers are comfortable themselves and don't even recognize that there is an issue that needs to be addressed:

I just don't think the men who are still largely running our organizations today see this as a problem. They don't see glass ceilings as a problem. They don't see the diversity issues that are happening at lower levels, because at their level it's not usually real apparent. They haven't had any problems [lawsuits] there.

Susan, the eldest of the group, dealt with much of the latent discrimination that Judy described, and had this to say when I asked if she thought she could have been the president of her company: *"I would never have gotten to be president. That would've been viewed as lack of respect for the legacy that many years had built."*

Only two of the Lost Leaders, Barbara and Pegge, feel that they were never discriminated against. They both worked in companies with strong affirmative action and diversity programs, which I believe helped to reduce the likelihood of more overt forms of discrimination. These two women did not, however, identify those programs as a reason for their positive experiences. Pegge is an engineer and worked in very male-dominated fields where she was often the only woman in a particular job but felt that *"in general, if you performed you had opportunity. And in general it was gender neutral. That's what you want. That's what you want."* Her company was a government contractor who had a track record of hiring and promoting a diverse workforce. These efforts were probably in place for many years when Pegge arrived in the early eighties, and she benefited from the resulting environment. This most likely influenced her personal opinions regarding discrimination:

I never—well personality exceptions, a few individuals—but in general, I never felt being a female in that field was a disadvantage. If we stop focusing on "poor me"or"I'm a woman therefore," and just focus on professionalism and exceptional results, even when there is a barrier, you break through it easily, easily. You know, good ol' boy in a manufacturing plant in the South, and they spit their wad of tobacco out before they shake your hand, to across the country, even when there would be a little of not being taken seriously, if I just focused on helping them solve problems, I'd do exceptionally well. So many people make the opposite mistake. If more women would think, "I can't change them but I can change how I let it affect me." Focus on being the best professional you can possibly be, which produces results, any barrier is going to be so temporary.

As positive as Pegge is about her ability to overcome obstacles, she does admit they exist. Words like "a little of not being taken seriously," indicate that some of the men she dealt with did subscribe to sex-role stereotypes, not believing that a woman can perform in a traditionally-male career like engineering. Pegge is sure she was able to overcome these initial impressions by "being the best professional." Her efforts may well have pushed the glass ceiling upward, as the men she encountered hopefully changed their opinions of women, because of their experience with her. Unless, of course, they just assumed she was an exception, different from other women.

Barbara's experience and personal philosophy are similar to those of Pegge. She recognizes that the structure of the corporation where she worked aided in creating the environment. She was more apt to acknowledge that gender discrimination occurs, but holds firm that she was not a victim of it herself, and does not feel that her former employer discriminated:

Could be, you know that big an organization, certainly, they put a lot of stuff in place, to avoid lawsuits. But I personally never observed or felt that I was discriminated against. Now, that's not to say that I did not observe or think there were good ol' boys, but to me that was their problem. Certainly, there would be statements of bias, just because I felt there are male chauvinist pigs, for lack of a better term, who worked there. But that was who they were; there were also lots of other kinds of people who worked there. For me it was always your performance. That was my perspective on it. I don't like affirmative action because I think that it's as discriminating as—you know, it should be based on one's performance, their merits, their capabilities ... and that's not to say that other people didn't feel it. But I think there's a whole problem with victimism in this world, where people simply don't take responsibility for their own lives and their own actions, who say, "I can't." And it's men and women, white, black, and Chinese, it doesn't matter. There are people in this world who fall on the victim side of the scale as opposed to the responsible side of this scale.

Like Pegge, Barbara acknowledges that there were barriers, "statements of bias." She also agrees with Pegge that if you don't take on the victim role you can succeed on merit. Barbara does admit that she may have benefited from the affirmative action program that she does not support:

I never felt it. And I don't think even in the reverse I haven't—yet may have. Well, when I was promoted to my first director position, I was the only woman. Maybe they felt compelled to bring a woman in because they had all these men. I don't know.

The experiences and opinions of these two women are important in the contrast that they provide to the stories of the other Lost Leaders. As I have speculated, their positive experiences may have been the result of years of affirmative action in their companies, although they clearly are believers in meritocracy. That they have managed to maintain this belief after many years in corporations may be evidence of the benefit of affirmative action, or may be purely a reflection of their worldview or their specific career experiences.

In all of the career stories the Lost Leaders shared with me, there is an element of individual experience of discrimination, but all of these women were high achievers, in spite of those experiences. They were selected for my research based on the fact that they had achieved a certain level of success in the corporate world; to do that in the timeframe covered here required that women be exceptionally well qualified and have higher than average willingness to persevere. When presented with the level of success the Lost Leaders experienced, many of them, as well as those who were watching them, found proof that things are getting better for women. I agree that things are better, partially because of the efforts and successes of the Lost Leaders. This does not excuse the blatant and latent discrimination they experienced. How many leaders have been lost well before they reached this level of success? How many more will be?

CHAPTER TEN

The Toxic Workplace

When the Lost Leaders reached the executive ranks, they had an insider's view of how American corporations are run. Many of their stories are of poor leadership—and the Lost Leaders were eventually tired of the constant demands to grow the business and increase short-term profits, regardless of the long-term impact on the company or the impact on the lives of employees. *Fast Company* magazine once proclaimed American businesses "toxic places to work."[1] The Lost Leaders would not disagree.

Strong opinions were expressed about the leadership at the very top of corporations. Of course, not all of the leaders were bad, but most of the stories recounted were negative, and this played a large part in why these leaders were lost to the corporate world. Here is an example from Barbara:

I think the politics that exist in companies—it just wastes a lot of energy. Doing things, not because it's right or wrong, but because of how it's going to position you, you know, for the next election. I don't think I worked for any company where at the very top I felt that there was really strong leadership that was taking the organization somewhere.

Nancy, who received good management training early in her career, observed that such skills are not common and often not even valued at higher levels:

There's a lot written about how to be supervisors and managers, but being presidents is something that they just assume people can do. In fact they can't. If anything, they turn into more jerks, because what happens

*is that the people you're managing are higher and higher up and not so
fragile. You know, when you are a frontline manager, people are more
likely to sue you, complain about you, than those higher up. It's kind of
expected (at the executive level) and I think that just by our nature, we put
up with more. It's much more unusual to hear about some vice president
or senior vice president who has some action against the company. Even
though the things companies do, in terms of sexism, are just as bad, if not
worse, at those levels. They just aren't careful anymore, because they don't
think they need to be.*

The values exhibited by leaders are a part of corporate culture and they are demonstrated, in part, by the way that people
are treated within the company. When Nancy was promoted to
senior vice president at Comp Sales, a *Fortune* 100 company, she
thought she had truly "made it," but she quickly found that her
boss, George, the new company president, had an abusive management style:

*He was not at all sexist. He was very progressive in that way, but basi-
cally a real son of a bitch. He cared about smart, hardworking people and
he happened to like me. When there was a senior vice president position
open, he talked to me about it and ultimately offered me the job. I was
on an incredible high, thinking of all I had accomplished. But within two
days I realized that he was a complete asshole, as far as being a boss—
horrible, horrible. I mean, I've had bad bosses, but he was just mean and
degrading to everybody who worked directly for him. He was so inept from
a management standpoint; it was his belief that he had to beat you up to
get the most out of you. So I immediately went into a sort of depression, if
you will, thinking: "What the hell did I get myself into?"*

Nancy went on to describe how she learned to survive in this
environment, and how it finally led to her decision to leave the
corporate world:

*Eventually, I realized that the only thing that worked with George was
to fight back. I don't like confrontation particularly; I certainly don't like
it in the workplace. The best working situations that I've ever had were
when I had a good relationship with my boss, when they counted on me.
I think George did count on me, but his style was to abuse you, because
that's how he knew you were passionate. So I would fight back with him*

all the time, because that's what he liked, how he gained respect for you. It was the sort of situation which can work if you can get used to going to the office sick to your stomach.

At one point, probably within a year of when I finally left, he pushed me too far. I was in his office, and his office was separated only by a conference room from the CEO's office; it was their own little suite. I was in his office and the door was open. I'm sitting there going over some things with him and he said something that just pushed my buttons, big-time. I started cussing at him! [laughs] Yelling and cussing at him. I said to him, "You're a f-ing asshole." I just went off; I'd never done that before. I lost my mind. I'm like, "You're an asshole." He's like, "I'm not an asshole." I'm like, "You are!" The secretaries are right outside, and, finally, the CEO appears at the door, and he said, "So, how's it going?" [laughs]. That was just enough. Obviously, you don't like being caught by your parents. It was just enough that we both stopped and looked at each other. I could just feel my blood pressure was probably maxxed out. The CEO talked for a few minutes about something else, distracted us.

Later I went back to my office and called my husband, and I said, "Well, I'm working on my severance package today" [laughs]. My husband said, "Oh, you have to go back and apologize to him." I said, "I can't apologize to him. That's what he's all about. He's all about power, and if I go back like a girly-girl and apologize to him I'm going to lose any feeling from him that I can stand on my own." Eventually I went and said to him, "You know, sorry I yelled at you, but you really did piss me off." I tried to take a masculine approach to it. In any case, after a few years of that, you just get sick of it.

Lest this be considered an isolated case, remember that, in an earlier chapter, Barbara shared her story about the toxic culture at the business that spun off from BGV. Here she characterizes the leader of the new company:

He will call people and swear at them and threaten to fire them, "Who made this big screw up?" and he's the CEO of this business. The culture followed the leader, which is a total lack of respect for people. There's just no respect for the people.

And Colleen, who worked nine years for Mercantile, a family-owned business, did not feel that *she* was treated like family, especially not on her last day when she was escorted from the building with no prior notice:

"We just want you out of here." The thing that bothered me a lot about that company was they presented themselves as, "Oh, we care about our people, we're family." And then they treat me the way they did, after years of hard, hard service and dedication.

Pegge felt that the major manufacturing company she worked for treated people well, but as part of her job she worked with supplier companies that did not. She describes her philosophy and that of her employer as an application of the golden rule:

If you are driving a customer service, customer-focused organization, first and foremost you have to treat people like you want them to treat the client. I say that and I worked very closely with other companies that were [suppliers] for products. One of the real challenges was that lack of professionalism, lack of core values in treating employees like you would want to be treated or like you would want the customer treated. It was use and abuse the employees, provide them no support, versus what I was in was more professionalism, respect for employees, treat them like you would want them to treat the clients, invest in them.

Nancy had experienced attempts by leaders of Comp Sales to create a better, more professional organization, but added that: *As soon as times got tough, they hunker down and turn back into assholes, which was their normal . . . and that's probably a charged word, but they turned back into sort of an onslaught of authoritative, autocratic, "good because I said so," type management style.*

Here she expands on how this evolved over time:

When I first came to Comp Sales it was a young, growing company. The first year I started there they had just made the Fortune 500. They were very fast and nimble, in fact, at that time. It was all about achieve-ment and more money and perks. A "work hard and play hard" sort of mentality. Everybody was young; senior managers were, in my mind, relatively inexperienced, from a management standpoint, but good at what they were doing, the business itself.

The company later started, when they were a little more mature, they wanted to start offering management training. Prior to that, they had no management training, no supervisory training. Now they had this "better self" that they were aspiring to and started offering a lot of things like training. But what I believe happened is they were only able to be their better self when times were great, you know, the whole land of milk and honey. When times were great, the stock was going up and people were getting rich. You had salespeople getting speedboats for bonuses, and lots of other perks for the sales staff. They had the ability, the luxury if you will, of spending money on things like training and trying to be their better self.

But, like many companies, as things started to contract, the first to go are the things which the company thinks they can live without. The first thing that they let go was management training and so forth, and then the whole ideal of management programs went by the wayside, because they became more desperate. My two cents is that the folks who had been there for a long time really didn't have any strong management experience, and really never were great managers. They were just paying lip service to it and training the people below them. I think there was a "better self" ideal, but it was only a part of the company when we had the luxury to do that. Once we didn't, it was the first thing to go.

It was a different place afterward. At the beginning, nobody really cared. You had kids with two years of college pulling down $100,000 a year in sales; it was "yeeha!" Nobody really cared about good management. But later, when you're contracting and laying people off, you're starting to push sales quotas that people had never even seen before, and then you tack onto it the dictatorial management behavior, that changed the whole culture, or the tone, the daily life of these folks.

Loyalty is also a value—loyalty of the employees to the company and of the companies towards their employees. The Lost Leaders felt that both had declined since previous generations or, for the older women, during their own careers. One manifestation of a lack of loyalty is high turnover. Many comments were made about high levels of turnover in a variety of different companies, but especially in the younger, more "maverick" companies.

Judy, who worked for the same organization for over 25 years, only to see herself and most of the long-tenured workforce offered "early retirement," finds that most executives she calls today in her executive recruiting business are open to talking to her about changing companies. They recognize that there is no job security:

The companies are the ones that aren't loyal. The workers of today have seen their parents, their grandparents, their sisters, brothers, laid off. We saw that across Corporate America, everyone has been touched by layoffs once, twice, five times.

The phenomenon of low levels of loyalty was sometimes attributed to a lack of commitment by a new generation of employees, but most of the Lost Leaders agreed that the "rightsizing" of workforces represents a lack of loyalty by businesses to their employees and led to this lower commitment. As Judy pointed out, being laid off can, and most likely will, happen to everyone who works for a large company, if it has not already.

Many of the problems that the Lost Leaders describe here are "toxic" for women and men alike. The Lost Leaders are a product of their environment, they know that competition and profit maximization are part of business, but they also value respect and loyalty, while the workplaces they describe appear to value them less and less. Mary Anne has built a consulting practice around coaching others on how to survive in workplaces that show many of these traits of being toxic. Here she shares the advice she gives to women within them:

In my coaching of women, I include being mindful of people trying to sabotage your success. That's just organizations. That's Corporate America. Everybody is vying for a place at the top and a special pat on the back, or something, from the CEO, and oftentimes women attack other women. I've seen a fair amount of that. I don't say a lot, but I've seen it. It's not uncommon. I think people are trying to get to the top, on their climb up the ladder, so to speak, and they will knock anybody out of the way that they deem a threat. I truly believe that's what motivates it. I think it's a power play.

When I'm coaching women, at the beginning, I say, "Let's survey the landscape and look for who could potentially threaten your success, and why might they want to. Let's look even deeper at where you're sitting and who all wants to be where you're sitting—around you, below you, even above you—who might fear that you could usurp their authority or come in and pose a threat to their power or their interests. Look at how we can minimize those threats or eliminate them." If there's a woman at the top who is very strong and dominant, and my coaching client is under that woman, or adjacent to her, somewhere in the organization, trying to succeed, my coaching is to be very mindful of that threat and the interests of that woman. Think about how you're dressing, think about what you're saying, think about who you're connecting with and networking with, and what your interests are, and how that might conflict with her interests. To the extent that you don't pay attention to those things, you're shooting yourself in the foot, and you're compromising yourself in terms of what you want to achieve. You have to be not only emotionally intelligent, but politically intelligent, and culturally intelligent.

This does not sound like common sense to me, it sounds a bit paranoid. But then, I left the toxic workplace behind years ago. Mary Anne also left it, and went on to share that this type of environment is a big part of why she left:

One of the reasons I'm working on my own now is because, even though corporations are changing and there are some extraordinary cultures out there, you still have to be very mindful of the political and cultural and social dynamics inside organizations, if you want to be successful. If you take your eye off the ball, man or woman, you are compromising your ability to achieve your goals of being successful. That, some people say, is playing politics. You can call it whatever you want, it is a very real thing, and you have to know how to read the unspoken language of the culture, to know how to navigate inside of it successfully, and, if you don't, you're going to get hurt. Somewhere in the game, you are going to get hurt. I have to do that with my corporate clients, in many ways, navigate their cultures and be appropriate when I'm inside them, dress appropriately, establish a presence appropriately, but I don't want to do that every day, all day. That's why I broke off on my own. I don't want to do that anymore.

Mary Anne seems to be trying to put a positive spin on the corporate workplace, despite the fact that she does not want to be part of it. It is difficult to know if Mary Anne really doesn't question the sanity of this type of environment, or if she is just trying to defend the workplaces that have provided her with a lucrative consulting business. She makes it clear, however, that she would not want to return to a corporate role herself.

In contrast, Judy did nothing to defend the corporate culture she believes pervades businesses today. She spent almost 30 years in one company as it grew and expanded, eventually becoming MegaBank. During her career she was part of the team that led MegaBank's efforts to be an inclusive workplace, that "better self" that Nancy spoke of, but eventually, Judy's company also succumbed to pressure to produce higher and higher profits. MegaBank changed so much, and cut so much staff and administration, that Judy could no longer support its goals. She felt that the progress she had been part of had been abandoned. She is among the eldest of the Lost Leaders—and is one of the most bitter. This bitterness is in spite of the fact that she left MegaBank with a pension plan, including healthcare, which left her financially independent at age 50. Perhaps her strong feelings are the result of giving so many years to the company, before finding much more satisfying work in her own business. Or perhaps she has just seen too much. This is how she summarizes her feelings now:

My personal belief is that business is run by men and they don't have a lot of women whispering in their ear about how it looks and how it's not right, and I think the dollar has driven people to do things that are a backstab to all the work and all the effort that went on in the 70s and 80s to work towards equal opportunity. When you look and see the numbers of women who are making it, and have made it, it's all typical. Most of the individuals are single. They work exponentially more than their male counterparts.

I think there's been a lot of lip service paid to the glass ceiling. I truly believe the glass ceiling has been bulletproofed. I don't think it's been permeated. Women are given a bunch of crap and they believe it. They drink the Kool-Aid. They drink the corporate Kool-Aid. They get handed a small little token. The corporate jet comes and takes them someplace and they have a lunch with somebody and they think that that's arriving. So they are given a crumb and they take it and they move on. They tell themselves, "Well, this is the way it is everywhere." When you are isolated, you don't really have a chance to compare like you did with your girlfriends in high school: "He told you that? He told me that, too, that…" I see some really smart women out there and I see them sitting in the same damn place that they were five years ago. It's okay if you stay in that as long as you know what the deal is, but you really are fooling yourself to think that it's changing because of you, it's not. I think that is the saddest thing.

Although she was at a very high level, as mentioned earlier, human resources is not a place of power, it is a supportive role. Judy was not comfortable supporting the policies that she did not feel were in the best interest of the employees. Now she focuses her executive search business on helping other corporate executives move out of big bureaucracies like MegaBank to smaller, more entrepreneurial companies, where she feels they will be treated better and their contributions will be more valued. Her rant here is as much a treatise against big business, with its emphasis on profits, as it is a cry for equality for women.

PART 3

Hopes for the Future

Despite their abbreviated corporate careers, the Lost Leaders have not stopped contributing to the economy. They have a desire to work and achieve; they have just given up on doing it within the corporate structure. Each has found a place to contribute, working as independent consultants, small business owners, or in key positions in smaller or less restrictive organizations. Their new roles have more flexibility and allow them more control over their lives and their own success. The stories of their new ventures were told with the enthusiasm that is a mark of good leaders. How much have corporations lost because the Lost Leaders are not leading them?

The Lost Leaders were surprisingly optimistic about the future for women in corporate workplaces. I asked them to think about what would need to change so that women who are in executive roles now and in the future could stay and succeed. Several women brought up the subject of a woman president of the United States—an important symbol that women can be trusted with big decisions. Others feel that the use of new technology could make things better, allowing more flexibility in work hours, leading to more balance for all workers. Some observed that the women and men of the generation now entering the workplace seem more resistant to restrictions of the ideal worker model. That alone may bring about changes, as businesses become dependent on this group, and they move into higher levels within organizations.

The ideas and reflections shared by these women should be taken to heart by those interested in creating a truly inclusive workplace, one where everyone with the talent and skill to lead can achieve their career goals within the corporate structure—one in which so many women will not give up their careers. The Lost Leaders all agreed on one thing—they would never go back to Corporate America. That is a tremendous loss to American business.

CHAPTER ELEVEN

Joy in Work

These women want to work. Although some have husbands who can support them and children to care for, they have not abandoned their careers or chosen full time parenting/homemaking. Yes, some of them wanted more flexibility so that they could enjoy those aspects of their lives, but they also enjoyed their jobs and want to be contributing to the world through work. They have invested years of their time and much energy into building their careers and want to continue to achieve.

The Lost Leaders used words like "interesting," "exciting," "learning," "contributing," "challenge," "making a difference," "feeling fulfilled," "valued," and even "fun" to describe times in their early careers that they were really happy. They used similar words when describing what they are doing now that they have left the corporate environment and are working more independently. When describing their reasons for being unhappy in the latter years of their corporate careers, they used words like "boring," "hard to make a difference," "don't have much control," "ideas not being heard," "lack of inclusion," "it wasn't fulfilling,"—and this was at the director and vice president levels. These examples provide evidence that the women desired the sense of accomplishment that they achieved when they felt they were really able to contribute to a corporation through their talents. Some are financially secure enough that they could stop working if they chose, but they do not seem interested in completely giving up this part of themselves. For example, Patricia, an ex-accountant, provided this quick analysis:

I could stop working; I don't really have to work. If we sell our beach house and roll the equity into our home, we could easily get by on my husband's salary.

But she also expressed this:

I want to work; I need that, it's just me. I want my sons to know that the mom has a life outside. I don't want them to think that my world revolves around them. It was nice to do that for a while during my time between jobs, but I feel good about working, doing cool stuff, and making money.

Nancy had not yet settled on a new career, but did not think she could give up working:

I think that a lot of the mental stimulation, challenge, helps to make you feel good about what you know, who you are, and I think at some point I would miss not having it.

The highest ranking of the women in this book, Nancy was also the most philosophical about her departure from the corporate world. She had a stay-at-home husband, so the work hours were never an issue for her, and her job required very little travel. She just could not support the company anymore. She had gotten close enough to the top to see that she did not respect the leaders and no longer felt satisfied in her work:

I had really gotten to the point where although the money was nice and all, it wasn't worth the unhappiness side of things. It's not about the hours or the work, because I think, at least for me, if you're fulfilled, if you're making a difference, if you're appreciated at least a little bit; you're appreciated by your boss anyway, the long hours and stress are okay. When you have an achiever type personality like I do, you can endure a lot of peripheral stuff, if you feel like you're getting back that sense of accomplishment and gratification. That was nowhere.

As someone who was able, and willing, to conform to the ideal worker model, Nancy's story demonstrates the importance of being valued for your contribution. Recall the story she told of her shouting match with a verbally abusive boss, the company president, in an earlier chapter. She left her career specifically for reasons based on a culture that did not allow her to achieve the satisfaction of contributing to the success of the business.

When I first met Colleen, she had gone through the emotional experience of leaving her job just a few days before. Here is how she described her early years at that company:

The first six years were absolutely insane, crazy. I was working 70- and 80-hour weeks, because I was building an internal advertising agency. It was such a great experience. I loved it, it was great.

By our third interview, she had spent time reflecting on her career and was more introspective about the entire experience and about her future:

The reason I'm leaving the corporate environment is because there was no balance in my life at all. I'm pretty much a workaholic, but now I just want to step back and try to understand how I can contribute to society, how I can hopefully make a difference somewhere, and make a living.

Divorced and childless, Colleen was also able to conform to the ideal-worker model, but tired of it. Once she was outside of the corporate environment, she realized that it had co-opted her. But she still wants to make a contribution.

The Lost Leaders recognize that their frustration level may be partly due to burnout after many years in the workplace, or just part of their current life-stage, but they also seek what work theorists have identified as "joy in work."[1] Most of the women had this joy, what they would call job satisfaction, early in their careers, but could no longer find it inside large businesses. Despite the seemingly powerful positions that they held, the women began to see that they had little power or control over their work lives. Being laid off, as several of them were, is the undeniable proof of this loss of control. They were also kept from achieving their career goals through blatant and latent forms of discrimination, as well as the inflexible environments and male-dominated culture—all of which caused them to feel powerless. This powerlessness also kept them from achieving "joy in work." Several have recaptured this feeling working as consultants and in smaller organizations. They do not want to abandon this part of themselves; they want to work, it is part of who they are.

Susan provides an interesting view of what is missing in corporate jobs; why she was not able to achieve the joy of work she needed in hers:

The biggest thing is what I call intellectual diversity. I relate it to multitasking. I was always bored in corporate jobs. No matter how challenging the job was, it wasn't broad enough in terms of diverse activities and diverse ideas. It was going to the same place, doing the same thing, working on the same work, day in and day out. That is what I refer to as lack of intellectual diversity.

When I was in the corporate environment, even though there were many things to do, filling in hours, it wasn't intellectually diverse. It wasn't like I could go from this problem today to this problem tomorrow and then go back to that problem yesterday with a fresh perspective. It was keep working on the same problem, over and over for the next 20 years. Even if you succeeded, it was still only one problem. That was the number one reason I chose not to go back into a full-time corporate position.

In my consulting practice, if I can't get something solved at one client, I'm probably going to see it at a different client, and then I can look at it from a different perspective. Maybe from what I learned over here, I can draw some analogies to something over there. I did not find a company where that was possible. It was the same process over and over. Sometimes the people change, but it was pretty much an environment with hundreds of years of history of "This is how we do it; this way."

I don't remember having a job that I wasn't bored at. And it's not like, you know, I'm not talking 162 IQ! [laughing] It was the repetition, the constants, the same expectations. There was nothing different and the expectations didn't change, because the culture says: "Here's how we solve problems. Here's the problem solving methodology that this company uses. We all use this. We all know it." If it was seven steps someplace else, it might be five steps here. You apply the formula to come up with the solution. Okay, next problem. So there's nothing truly different or genuinely intellectual about it.

Nancy spoke of what she will do next, and is hopeful that she will have more time with her children but also find meaningful work. She recognizes that having choices and options is a luxury that most women do not have. She is afforded this opportunity because of the rewards of the work she has done in corporations, but does not wish to continue to the next level:

I have young children now, and I think I'm in a position that a lot of women are not, because I've already had a big enough career. There was lots of money and it's given me the ability to actually think, "Would I rather have a life with my children?" Most people can't make that choice, but I can. I don't really know how it will all work out. I'm going to be 47 this year, and I've got a five-year-old and an eight-year-old. I think, when you're older and financially comfortable, sometimes you sit back and say "What's really important?" and "What do I feel like doing?" I really think I'd like to enjoy my kids' lives, while they're still home with me. Once they are grown, I'm not averse to work. At the same time, I don't need to do it 50 or 60 hours a week. I don't want to be just driven by my screwed-up need for achievement. I want to make the right decision for me. I don't feel like I have anything to prove any more.

Nancy is struggling with her decision. At the time of this interview she was working in an educational institution. She thought the academic environment would be better than what she had experienced working in large corporations, but it had its own set of challenges. Although she is willing to sacrifice financial rewards to have more time with her children, she struggles because she still thrives on achievement. Why should she have to give up one for the other? Why should anyone?

CHAPTER TWELVE

Free Agency

In his first book, Daniel Pink identified the phenomenon of the *Free Agent Nation*. He describes "free agents" as those who have left corporations and taken charge of their lives, becoming what he categorizes as soloists, temps, or owners of micro-businesses.[1] Most of the Lost Leaders are now soloists, selling their talents to corporations as consultants. Nancy, while undecided on her future path, was at least sure of this:

Not to work for somebody else is my real preference. I would probably be most viable as a consultant in my own field. But with all that I've done—I've cooked for a living, I've worked in factories and managed gas stations, worked in nursing homes—that has told me that there's a lot of things I can do. I don't just have to stay on the same path I'm on now. I'd much rather do something totally different, something like buy houses and fix them up and sell them or something. I'd like to do something like have a coffee shop/bookshop if you could make a living at it. I'd like to do something where I didn't have to be involved with the bowels of corporate. I could end up doing nothing other than finding a way to make money without having to go to an office all the time. I'm really looking for something with more freedom.

Joan Williams, who wrote extensively on the challenge of the ideal worker model, considers this phenomenon among women to be evidence of the abilities and creativity that they have been unable to use inside corporations.[2] The reasons the women give for making the choice of self-employment include a desire for flexibility, as well as just being tired of trying to assimilate, and of trying to please leaders who they no longer respect. Yet, as discussed in the previous chapter, they still want to work, they want to be productive, and they enjoy the new roles they have carved out for themselves. This is how Judy, who has built a successful business in executive recruitment, describes the phenomenon, in her usual, frank manner:

The number of women who have started their own businesses or who are working in businesses that are primarily owned by women has jumped exponentially. I would say two to three hundred percent, because women today are tired of the male-dominated corporate environment. They're tired of the rhetoric. They're tired of doing more work and getting less money, or doing equal work and getting less money. They're tired of being left behind, not being included, when they know they are making a difference. So they are saying, "Okay, if I feel this way, I'm going to at least try starting my own business."

Joyce observed this about flexibility in the workplace, based on her research for a book on the topic of work–life balance:

I saw way more creativity [regarding work–life balance] in the entrepreneur ranks. Those women were feeling it directly, so they were more likely to be aware of or more sensitive when their employees needed it. But maybe it's an entrepreneurial thing in general, because I look at my husband who has his own business and if his employees need to take off, he doesn't think twice about it. I think you can be more flexible and more adaptable. I'm not going to say it is that way in all small businesses, but that is where I think the creativity and innovation is coming in terms of how to structure work. If you are going to be an entrepreneur, you have to have a certain chutzpah and a certain willingness to look at things differently, and you're small enough that you can adapt. If you want a certain person to work for you, you are more willing to do what it takes to keep them happy. You may not necessarily be able to pay them as much, so maybe the flexibly or similar types of things are ways to entice them.

In the next chapter, The Balancing Act, the Lost Leaders speculate on how some of the benefits of self-employment could be made available in the corporate workplace. Mary Anne, who argued that many women still love their jobs on the inside of companies, was clear that she herself would not go back to corporate: *I like working at my desk in jeans and T-shirts and flip-flops when I want to. I like taking off at noon for the rest of the day just because I feel like it. And I might work Sunday morning, get up at seven, and work till noon on Sunday. That's okay, I can, and I can sort of create my own culture, if you will, for a large part of my work. I like that. The flip side is I have a lot of risk. I don't have a paycheck coming in every two weeks. So I have to manage the risk of running my own business. That's okay for me. It's well worth it.*

A woman who recently started her own advertising agency told me that she is surprised when people ask her if she is worried about the lack of security. Being a corporate employee, in her opinion, was much less secure. She, at least, has some control over her future. Patricia gave this rousing endorsement for leaving corporate life behind:

What will I do now? Well, I am done with Corporate America. Absolutely. You can stick a fork in me; I'm done. It's just not good for me. I'm just not good at it: managing up, kissing up, playing politics. I just want to work.

I just think when you're smart and you have energy, I think you can make a lot more money and have a lot more freedom, if you work for yourself, or a very, very small company. My husband is an example, he works managing this building his family owns. He spends an average 15 hours a week but makes three-quarters of what he was making before in a corporate job. He says that, literally, you work as much, but in corporate you have to add in all the bullshit meetings and bullshit in the hallways, he thinks he's actually working about the same amount of hours. And that's why I don't want Corporate America. I'm not bitter. It was just off the handle. I am thankful for every experience, it got me to where I am now, but I don't want to do anything where half of my time is not adding value. I just want to add value and go home and go on vacation and get rest and have more free time.

Susan, who left corporate primarily because of the travel, took control of her own destiny and started a consulting business. She has built a professional reputation and manages to find plenty of work without ever getting on an airplane. Now that her practice is thriving, she laughs that self-employment means you get to pick which 23 hours a day you work. She also admits that she has not had a vacation since her honeymoon over five years ago. Despite the hours, and although she has had many attractive offers, she has resolved never to return to traditional employment.

Colleen, who was still in transition, has reached the conclusion that she will most likely end up self-employed in some form:

I don't want to sound like an eternal pessimist, but I really believe that if you want an honest, truthful working environment, you have to make it yourself. There is not a lot of honesty at the top for me to believe in anymore. I don't want to sound like a scorned woman or anything, but I think for me, at this next level in my life, I'm looking for that truth. I'm wanting to be a part of something good, something strong, but also something truthful. If I can't find it, I'm going to create it myself.

Colleen is one of the older women in this book. She started her search for a career when there were truly no public role models for women. But Colleen, as you recall, had the model of her mother and other strong women in her family. Perhaps it was this strength that led her to refuse to back down once she had established herself in her specialty, advertising. Perhaps it was this strength that was met with resistance from the young male leaders she spoke about in the part 2. Her reflections here came just three months after her corporate career ended abruptly. She took that time to recover and begin to develop a new plan for her life. Here is how she views the corporate workplace after this short time out of it.

I don't think you can fix Corporate America. I think what we have to do is create a new business model of our own. We can't tear down so much of that structure that has been built over so long and there are also so many attitudes and old mores that just won't go away right now.

While inside the structured corporate environment, people tend to have a skewed perspective of the financial benefit of having steady paychecks. Joyce told of a "back-of-the-envelope" calculation that gave her permission to leave her corporate job and start her own business:

I know that most people can't just say, "I've had enough. I'm out of here," but I was married and my husband and I, at that time, both made roughly the same amount of base salary. When we first talked about it: Could I leave? Could I go out on my own? Could I do something else? I did a back-of-the-envelope calculation. I said, "Okay, let's start with what my W-2 says I make." Then I backed out all the taxes, which were pretty significant because of the marriage penalty in the tax rates at the time. My income pushed us into a higher tax bracket, so I could back that out, and I started detailing all of the work-related expenses. I added up the dog walker, paying for suits and other dress clothes that I wouldn't need if I could work in a different way, eating breakfast out every day, eating lunch out every day, ordering takeout or eating out most nights during the week, because we were too tired to cook, and on and on and on. The occasional massages or shopping therapy, because I was so frigging stressed, all the dry cleaning, the alterations, the gasoline back and forth. So what was the bottom number? The bottom line once I backed all that out?

My first reaction was: I was ready to cry and be pissed all at the same time, because I was literally killing myself. My body was literally shutting down, and that's all my family is benefiting? You think you're making a lot, but it basically came down to two really good vacations a year, is what it gives you. My first reaction was anger and sadness and the second reaction was, "Wow! I can make that number way easier in a lot of other ways that don't cause me nearly the brain damage." So all of a sudden, I had this freedom. That calculation gave me the freedom to move.

Judy gave this as her "bottom line:"

So the reality is that if I had a daughter starting out, the advice I would give her is to get a good education and find something that you have a passion about, and figure out who is really good, and do an internship or work for that person, then start your own business. That's what I would say.

For this generation of executive women, becoming Lost Leaders—leaving to find work of their own—is often the best option for their own personal growth and well-being, but it is not the best thing for businesses. If corporations truly want to keep women, they have to change their cultures or the women will continue to leave, and advise their daughters to do the same.

CHAPTER THIRTEEN

The Balancing Act

Flexibility was one of the most important reasons that the Lost Leaders chose self-employment. Corporations should consider accommodating such flexibility if they want to stop losing such high-potential employees. Joyce, in her book on work–life balance, studied various alternative work arrangements, and expanded on them with her own opinion:

There was one study of the women who left corporate jobs to go start their own companies. I don't remember the percentage, but it's significant. They left because they could not get the flexibility they wanted and needed at a traditional job. It would be nice if there was more flexibility, especially now that you can work from anywhere, why can't you just telecommute some of the time?

This flexibility, being able to control your own schedule, is something that several women felt was key to making the work-place more hospitable, especially for working mothers. Another woman I interviewed struggled with this her entire career:

If they gave you flextime—if I wouldn't feel guilty because I had to go to my kid's program, because then you're dealing with this guilty conscience. I'm guilty because I'm not working for my company, who's paying me and put some faith in me that I'm going to get this job done. And I feel guilty because I'm not with my kids.

Joyce and Patricia gave examples of flexibility provided by small business run by their husbands in the last chapter. In my own business, I was able to hire a much stronger team than I could otherwise afford, because I was flexible in their work schedules. The first woman I hired was married to a retiree and wanted to have more time to spend with him. She also had family overseas and needed extended time off to visit them once a year. Although it was a challenge for my small start-up to keep things moving when she was not in the office, she was extremely loyal and willing to take less pay as a trade-off. This helped me get started when funds were very limited. A few years later, another employee, my sales manager, had her first child. She wanted to continue to work but also wanted time with her baby. We worked out a part-time schedule that allowed her to work mostly from home. Given the key relationships she had developed for the business, being able to keep her connected prevented what could have been a destructive loss of momentum. She, too, became very loyal, putting in extra effort to show that she was able to maintain focus while working at home. My business benefitted greatly by allowing these two strong contributors the flexibility they desired. I was not doing it to make a statement about my belief in work–life balance; I felt that my business would not have had the same success if I had chosen two different people for these key positions, just because they were available on a more standard schedule or for more hours.

Technology has provided many people with increased flexibility in their work hours and the ability to work at home. The rapid changes that are occurring through the intensive use of technology enabled Colleen to envision a completely different kind of workplace:

I think that communication and what's going on in the world is going to recreate the business environment on its own in the next decade. I think the office as we know it will go away because of the connectivity. And once that happens and managers at the top lose control, they don't bring anybody into a room, what happens then? I think that that is going to force the next evolution in the business world.

The fact that this has not yet occurred may be evidence of the resiliency of the standard "office hours" model. Some would argue that the connectivity Colleen refers to has only extended the workday, taking over what had been left to the employees for

their personal lives. But the potential is there to utilize technology in a positive way to increase flexibility and give people more
control.

Joyce, after her study of work life a decade ago, does not feel
that corporate workplaces are ready to embrace flexibility, and
gave this example:

*My boss at Top Tier was phenomenal at doing his work while he was
there and being focused. He had an amazing ability to see all kinds of
crud, sort through it, and get right to the heart of it. He did that so he
could leave at five to go home and be with his family. For years he had
done that and had been successful, had done phenomenally well. Then
his product line had a downturn and the general manager said overtly,
"I don't think this works at the director level." He implied that if you
want to be successful, higher up the chain, you can't work regular hours.
That's for the people at lower levels. It's an attitude. I remember when I
interviewed people for my book, some of the managers would say, "Look,
we have flexible work programs on the books. What more do we have to
do? If people want to use them, they're there to use them." But if you
want to be taken at all seriously, if you don't want to be cut in the next
round of cuts, there was this underlying culture that frowned upon using
those things. The managers looked at it as, "That's the employee's own
individual problem; that's not my responsibility as a manager at the
company."*

Susan is more hopeful for the future, at least for the men who
want to make family a priority:

*I don't see a favorable climate for women; I don't see that necessarily
changing. What I see is a favorable, changing climate for the men who
have started saying, "I want to be home with my family." Women a
long time ago decided they couldn't change it. Company policies on using
technology and less travel and all of that didn't change until the men starting asking for it. I have men friends who are holding as firm as I used
to that, "I can't travel this week because . . ." and they're being regarded
for that. They have begun to change policies like travel. I would suggest
that for economic reasons companies are much, much leaner and therefore
travel budgets are smaller now. I would challenge in this day of technology,
whether the level of travel is so critical.*

Susan also shared her thoughts about what might drive a culture change in the types of workplaces where she struggled to fit in:

I think that with all the focus on innovation and fast cycle time, fast to the market and all that, I've seen that you can't have as much structure. Maybe this is just me being hopeful, I'm going to be naïve or Pollyannaish about it here, but it seems to me that, in this day of recognized need for innovation, that need implies, in my mind, the eroding of formal structure. I think the continued emphasis on innovation is a very positive thing for changing culture. I think a residual benefit, an unintended benefit, will be a more family friendly, a more life-balanced environment. If innovation gets rewarded, people will figure out how to be innovative, or they will hire people that are innovative, and innovation doesn't have a face, or a skirt or a pair of pants.

Colleen used the same "no skirt" description to expand on her "no office" model, above:

What will be beautiful about that is you don't have to come in and they don't care if you wear a skirt or a pantsuit. It won't matter because they can't see you. So hopefully that will begin to help.

Colleen emphasizes the benefits of not seeing the other person, not knowing if she is male or female, perhaps, at least not knowing if she has assimilated to the appropriate dress code. But implied here, and mentioned by others, is the fact that the workplace will becomes less structured, managers will have less control, and people can be free to achieve in their own way. The Lost Leaders felt that these changes would lead to increased emphasis on results and reduced importance of relationships. They are hopeful this will lessen the influence of the old boys' network.

Although many of the women brought up the issue of inflexible work hours or the need to be seen in the office, "face time," as problems, they did not hold much hope for a solution to this within the current corporate structure. As discussed previously, workplace flexibility and work–life balance are terms that have been tied specifically to the needs of women. Because of the strong cultural bias against them, women who want to be successful, especially as executives, have tended not to take advantage of policies that were supposedly written to help them. As Joyce shared above, using them was "frowned upon." Until men also demand flexibility and the ability to have time both for their work and their personal lives, these policies will not save the Lost Leaders. Susan's time away from corporate roles has given her the opportunity for reflection, and her work as a consultant provides a unique perspective. She was able to propose this as an optimistic solution:

Maybe you don't make it female friendly, maybe you make it family friendly. As more and more men become more balanced in their personal life around family, then it's not a matter of male versus female, it's a matter of that holistic approach to family friendly.

Joyce was able to share an example where a male leader had personal experience with what is traditionally the role of the working mom and was consequently more supportive of "family friendly" policies:

I know one company that was considered a shining example. They had a lot of policies in place and seemed to actually be using them. I remember hearing their CEO speak at one point. His wife was also a high-powered executive, and they would take turns driving the kids to daycare or school. One day he got to work and realized his toddler was still in the backseat, and he had to turn around. That company was more committed to having work–life policies in place and actually creating a culture where people felt like they could use them, because a senior officer was facing those issues himself. I don't work there, so I can't speak from being inside of it, but at least they talked a good game.

Legal feminists at the Center for WorkLife Law at the University of California Hastings College of the Law have chosen to focus on cases involving "family responsibility discrimination" as a way to emphasize that the issue is not specifically to benefit women or even just parents. Focusing on family responsibility, particularly in this era of "family values," is an excellent way to challenge that cultural norm. But for this chapter on balancing, I will give the last word to Joyce, the Lost Leader who is herself a work–life balance expert:

I think so much of it is top-down. The senior guys, and I say guys because it's almost all white males, they have to believe in work–life balance.

CHAPTER FOURTEEN

A Paradox of Diversity

Businesses have spent billions of dollars on initiatives designed to assist them in dealing with an anticipated increase in the "diversity" of their workforces.[1] When I began the research for my dissertation, I wanted to find out whether or not these corporate "diversity initiatives" had, or could have, any effect on the environment that kept the Lost Leaders from succeeding. This led to the title of my dissertation: "A Paradox of Diversity: Billions Invested, but Women Still Leave."[2] Unfortunately, the women's interviews did not provide much insight into these programs. The fact that these former executives had very little to say about them, is evidence in itself that diversity initiatives in corporations have not had a tremendous impact.

Over the years, diversity programs have often been poorly done or done merely so that the company can say they had been done. Consequently, they have sometimes done harm instead of good and led to skepticism regarding their potential effectiveness. Before the Lost Leaders share their views on this subject, some historical perspective is needed.

Corporate diversity programs trace their beginnings to a US Department of Labor report issued in 1987. The "Workforce 2000" report predicted that, by the year 2000, only 15 percent of net additions to the labor force would be white males.[3] Rapid growth of corporate diversity initiatives began with this prediction. At the beginning, diversity programs were limited to addressing race and gender, but the definition has broadened, first to include other groups protected by law such as age, religion, and physical ability, and later to add such factors as differing educational backgrounds, personality types, and family situations. Unlike affirmative action programs, diversity programs recognize that merely hiring a diverse workforce is not sufficient, something more is needed to ensure that those workers will stay and succeed.

Early forms of diversity training emerged from a 1960s "encounter group" model. Sometimes called sensitivity training, elements of such programs are still seen. The "plural" organization was typical of this early period; companies were starting to accept "others" but expected them to conform and assimilate to the predominantly white male workplace.[4]

In the early 1990s, diversity experts began to move away from the "plural" organization model toward a "multicultural" one that recommended against requiring individuals to assimilate into the dominant culture, but instead be allowed to bring their own views and experiences to the workplace.[5] To sell these programs, consultants told companies that they could increase profits by matching the demographics of their workforce with those of their customers.[6] Elements of this approach can sometimes be found in practice today. It has been criticized by social scientists because it often relies on "trait lists," which can actually lead to increased stereotyping.[7] Where this approach is taken, minority workers, and women have often ended up clustered in parts of the business where they could be "matched" to customer demographics, but not given any real power within the organization, and where they were not likely to be promoted to positions of power.[8]

More recent programs have kept some of the elements of multiculturalism, but have added a "business case for diversity." The business case holds that there is economic value in diversity through increased creativity and diverse viewpoints in decision making. Proponents also argue that there can be cost savings from reduced absenteeism and turnover, as well as from reduced discrimination complaints for businesses that undertake diversity initiatives. In addition, diversity is claimed to lead to business growth through understanding diverse markets, increasing creativity and innovation, enhancing leadership effectiveness, and building effective global relationships.[9] One business leader has been quoted as saying that the "business case for diversity" was needed because "moralistic statements, and race and gender militancy, would not sell diversity management to CEOs...[it] must be sold as business, not social work."[10]

Although they were not opposed to the current forms of diversity initiatives, the Lost Leaders were skeptical that they would be successful in the businesses where they themselves had tried to build careers. Judy was the only one who had extensive experience in this arena. She worked in human resources at a large corporation that had undertaken extensive efforts in diversity. The others had experienced very little in regard to diversity initiatives, which is evidence that there is really very little being done. The majority of the "billions" reported as spent is either being spent by a select few large corporations, or is misclassified from other areas, such as sexual harassment awareness or affirmative action. It may also be due to the fact that many companies use one-time, brief seminars that, although expensive when given to many employees, do not leave any lasting impression on the participants. A few of the women remembered attending diversity training, but could not recall anything specific about it.

Despite Judy's extensive experience with diversity programs, she was negative about their overall effectiveness. She expressed disappointment that the programs she helped to build had been all but abandoned when new management took over MegaBank. She does not feel that these programs can really change the deep-seated prejudice that she saw within its new, male-dominated, management team:

For many, many years, particularly in the 1980s, and into the early 1990s, I think we made tremendous strides. But MegaBank started getting pressure from Wall Street in terms of making the huge amounts of money that the investors had been used to. Then I think that the leadership took the easy road. The easy road was to cut positions, and the majority of the people that were cut were the women who were about ready to push through or make some real inroads into the next level or two of management. I think this happened in all industries.

I really did believe that we were going places and doing things and I really saw that there were some people that came along and really got on board with promoting a diverse workforce. The reality is that most of that progress has been undermined because of the fact that it wasn't followed through on. When somebody sees that, they know it's not important, and they don't act like it's important.

I think that the reality of the diversity movement is that it looks really good on paper. It sounds really good to say you are a worker friendly business and you have all these diversity programs. Peel back the onion and look at what the numbers say. Who are the female role models and are they at the table with the big boys? Do they socialize with them? Are they in the inner sanctum? The answer in my humble opinion is very, very, very rarely, if at all.

Organizations have all the right buzzwords, whether it's sensitivity training or diversity initiatives or inclusionary management style, but if the individuals don't really believe that women are as smart and capable as men, then you can have thousands of different programs and training sessions and none of those are going to work—if people innately don't believe that women are created equal.

Joyce worked for five years in the corporate headquarters of Top Tier, a very large, well-established company. Top Tier gets a lot of press for being a good place for women to work, but Joyce could only cite one session that she remembered as being overtly diversity training. She could not recall that seminar's content, but she was familiar with diversity programs through her research for a book on work–life balance and she shared her personal opinion:

Unless you're going to address the culture and structure of a company, it is difficult to expect change. There is definitely more pressure to assimilate to the company's culture. The programs were there so that they could say they were there.

In attempting to come up with a recommendation for the future, Joyce fell back to her beginnings in finance:

The only way to really get through to those guys at all will be financial. I've started developing an idea of the "lifetime value" of an employee: how much you've invested. Not just the turnover and finding a replacement, the investment in a person over time. I do think there is a financial case to be made. Some leaders will say, "I am an officer of this company. I am obligated to deliver results to the shareholders. That's who I'm tied to." You have to make the financial case, so they can go to their board and say, "This is why we can afford this."

Mary Anne, who has done extensive consulting in organizations, agreed that a financial motive is needed to interest leaders, especially those who deny there is a problem that needs addressing:

A lot of leaders in organizations, predominantly men, don't think there's an issue, so why spend all the money? There's nothing showing us we're going to get any great return, and we don't really have an issue anyway.

Nancy entered the workforce in 1975 as a 16-year-old high school dropout. She worked for some large companies before she obtained her college credentials and began her professional career. She acknowledged that the sensitivity training version of diversity programs was still in place when she started her career. She still feels that diversity initiatives are important, though she does not think they have made a major difference over her 30 years in the workplace. When I asked Nancy if she felt such programs were worth continuing, considering the low impact they seem to have had, she responded:

I think you have to continue to do them. Young people today have made some significant strides. Depending on what culture you come from, from your background, and where else you worked, that determines whether you really are sort of gender blind when you reach the workplace. You cannot say it's not better today than it was in 1960 when you never saw anybody in a position like mine that was female. There have been huge strides made. But I think to keep that going you have to keep, as they say, pushing the envelope, exposing people to things that are working in other companies, exposing them to new ideas, and I think the results will come.

The Lost Leaders' stories also provide some support for affirmative action programs. As discussed in part 2, Barbara and Pegge were the most positive about their corporate experiences and they were also the only two women who worked in companies where there were strong affirmative action policies. By the time these two women entered the workforce, their companies' compliance with affirmative action seems to have actually changed the way that women were being treated. I hesitate to make a broad generalization about the effectiveness of affirmative action based on the small number of women here, but this does provide some insight into how a company might be different because of it. Judy and Susan, on the other hand, worked for employers that were subject to these federal requirements, but did not embrace them. The culture of the organization is an important factor, and the attitudes of the leaders, whether they believe the policies are important, or that they just need to comply superficially, determines whether a policy will be effective.

The diversity initiatives that are being done today are vastly improved from earlier models that were criticized for raising negative emotions and perpetuating stereotypes. Professional consultants that are respected in this field design programs that include awareness training and skill building. Awareness training educates managers about the history of discrimination and the impact of stereotyping. Skill building allows trainees to practice utilizing their new knowledge. When these programs are done well, by qualified facilitators, it is possible to begin to change the overall culture in an organization, by exposing individuals to new ideas that can lead to changes in their attitudes and behaviors.

In order to address the problems faced by the Lost Leaders, diversity training must specifically address gender. One key goal of all diversity programs is to reduce stereotyping; male/female stereotypes can be part of that discussion. As discussed previously, our culture tends to view men as "heroic providers" and women as "nurturing caretakers," roles that can interfere with women reaching leadership positions in corporations. Diversity initiatives can address why the same behaviors are interpreted so differently based on gender. For example, when a woman puts her career first, hiring a nanny, so she can work long hours away from her children, she is vilified as a bad mother. If a man works long hours, seldom seeing his kids, he is admired as a good provider, making sacrifices for his children. Gender roles are a cultural norm that can be challenged by diversity programs.

In addition to quality training by qualified facilitators, these initiatives must have support of CEOs to be effective and their focus must be on changing the culture at all levels of the organization, as Joyce so aptly expressed:

You can put all the policies in place, but if the senior people don't buy into it, the culture won't change, because everyone takes their lead from that.

CHAPTER FIFTEEN

A Woman President of the United States

Three of the Lost Leaders independently brought up the topic of a woman president of the United States, when asked about their hopes for the future. This was before Hillary Clinton's historic run for the presidential nomination. Overcoming the perception that women are not capable of the highest office in our government was seen as an important symbol that would help to create a work environment where women would no longer be viewed as less capable than men. Judy, who was the most negative regarding the current state of the workplace, was the most vocal on this issue:

My optimistic view is there will be a woman president. There will be a woman president, I really hope in my lifetime. And when there is a woman president she will obviously select a lot of other women in roles and tasks and I think the ability to get things done, the ability to multitask, the ability to move it to the next level is going to be like Superman. Because once women have the power and once there is belief in this country that good things can happen and women do know how to handle things like economy and environment and war and famine and healthcare and all those factors and that we are making true inroads, we are not talking about the same issues 50 years from now, then I think we are really going to thrive.

In my humble opinion, you almost need a true huge leader that has a major voice and major power and all eyes will be upon her and a lot of doors will be open because the key that opens all the doors is that position. I've talked to a lot of women in business that are of the same mindset and age group that I am and almost invariably every single woman has said this to me: "I will vote for any woman that gets on the ballot over a man, any woman." That's how fed up women are with the lack of progress. We've been talking about the same issues for all the many, many, many years that men have been in office.

Judy not only thinks a woman as president will be symbolic, she feels it will change public policy so that we can put some important issues behind us for good. I found it interesting that her optimistic view is that a woman in leadership will be like Super*man*.

Nancy was not as philosophical as Judy, but also felt the lack of a woman in this role is a problem for women:

How stupid it is that the United States is not ready for a woman in the White House? I mean, that is just so stupid. For those of us who are professional women, we just sort of shake our heads at that.

And Colleen was also anxious for this seminal change in government:

I think what is sad is that we don't have enough women leaders. If we find somebody that could be president of the United States I'd go to work for her right now.

Most of the Lost Leaders felt that executive women have to be as much like a man as possible, without crossing that undefined line that might offend the men. Because of this, they expressed belief that women who have stayed and risen to the top have assimilated into the prevailing masculine culture and are either unwilling or unable (or both) to change it. How a woman who has succeeded in those circumstances could act differently after reaching the United States Presidency is an interesting question. This does not, however, undermine the symbolic importance of a woman in this powerful position.

CHAPTER SIXTEEN

Conclusion

It's time we stopped pretending that the barriers that kept women from reaching the top of America's corporations no longer exist. Yes, things are better than they were when the Lost Leaders first entered the workplace, but progress seems to have slowed. And yes, there have been some high-profile, successful women, but they are the exceptions. For most women, the barriers are still very real. As the infamous congresswoman Bella Abzug said in the late 1970s, and I echo today: "We don't want so much to see a female Einstein become an assistant professor. We want a woman schlemiel to get as quickly promoted as a male schlemiel."[1]

In the introduction to this book, I shared the story of a young female engineer whose boss recently said to her, "Working moms don't get promoted here." The problem, clearly, has not been solved. Unless, of course, you think that people should *have* to choose between career and family responsibilities. Is that what our society demands? In the words of Patricia Alexander, "Can we not procreate?!" That young female engineer—a highly educated, high-potential employee—has effectively been written off by her employer. Can we afford to waste talent in this way?

When the Lost Leaders *were* willing to adapt to the requirements of the ideal worker, when they *did* prioritize career over family, they have still been stopped from reaching the top. Whether it be due to a "glass ceiling," or the "old boys' network," those with the power to hold them back have made incorrect assumptions about their capabilities and commitment.

I chose, "The Lost Leaders," as the title for this book to empha-size the loss of talent to businesses, to remind us that the work-place issues discussed here are not just "social" issues, things that are unfair or unjust, or even illegal. The women here, and many more like them, have left the corporate world. Could this loss of leadership talent be a contributing factor to the stories of poor leadership—the ethical breaches and errors in judgment—that have dominated the business news in the past few years? Are America's corporations being led by the best and brightest of their generation? These are questions I feel are worth considering.

Corporations are now trying to regain the strength American business was once known for and struggling to re-earn the confi-dence of investors. Strong leaders are needed more than ever. The pool from which leaders are chosen now includes only those who were willing to make the "sacrifice" of time with their families and put up with treatment that, as described here, is very often inappropriate and sometimes less than humane. Although some leaders today are surely great human beings, they apparently don't believe there is another organizational model that allows busi-nesses to succeed. Many will argue that the global business envi-ronment does not allow for such "luxuries" as work–life balance. I think it is time to challenge that viewpoint, especially given the cost to business of losing a large portion of their leadership pool.

In addition to this loss of leaders for business, there are impor-tant social issues at play here. Given the depiction of the workplace as presented by the women in this book, we might ask ourselves if this is what we want American culture to be—the treatment of women as less than men, the wild fraternity-party atmosphere, the focus on short-term profits regardless of the long-term con-sequences for both business and families. I believe that American business culture can and will change—indeed, culture is always changing—and it may still be possible for us to live up to the ideal, what we aspire to be, what we say we already are: fam-ily friendly, with equal rights for all and respect for people—a corporate culture that does not require giving up your soul. Such a change would benefit both future generations and the families of today—the children who are being raised by the current generation of corporate executives.

One of my goals in writing this book was to bring the voices of the women into the discussion, to personalize it. Too often we talk about issues like "workplace discrimination" or "gender equity" in abstract terms. That academic approach is too easy—it ignores the lives and careers that are impacted by the behaviors and decisions within corporations. Oral history helps to illuminate the human side of social issues. The women's voices also demonstrate their competence—the leadership potential that has been lost.

So, what is a woman to do?

If there is one point that I want to make in this book, it is that women cannot solve this problem for themselves. The self-help books of the 1980s and 1990s that focused on what women could do to succeed, "fixing the women," followed by the many biographies celebrating the careers of successful women, have done little to address the issue at the heart of the matter. The environment of the corporate workplace, the culture that exists for managers and executives, needs to change. This includes the policies that value "masculine," "heroic" behaviors (but only in men) and those that equate commitment and competence with working long hours. Those who currently hold the power to change things must recognize that change is needed. My hope is that this book helps them to see the world from the viewpoint of the Lost Leaders, as a first step towards beginning the long process of changing the culture within their organizations.

Not every woman (or man) is qualified or seeks a leadership role, but those who have what it takes and the desire to lead should at least have a chance of being chosen. In the struggle to "have it all," everyone is losing: Women. Men. Families. Corporations. America.

NOTES

Introduction

1. Catalyst, "Latest Catalyst Census Shows Women Still Not Scaling the Corporate Ladder in 2010; New Study Indicates Clue to Reversing Trend," (media announcement, www.catalyst.org, 2010).

Part 1   Accidental Careers

1. William H. Whyte Jr., *The Organization Man* (New York: Anchor Books, 1956).
2. Daniel H. Pink, *Free Agent Nation: How America's New Independent Workers are Transforming the Way We Live* (New York: Warner Books, 2001).

Part 2   Corporate America

1. Joan Acker, "Hierarchies, Jobs, Bodies: A Theory of Gendered Organizations," *Gender & Society* 4, no. 2 (1990): 139–158; Sharon Bird, "Welcome to the Men's Club: Homosociality and the Maintenance of Hegemonic Masculinity," *Gender & Society* 10, no. 2 (1996): 120–132; and Jeff Hearn and David Collinson, "Men, Masculinities and Workplace Diversity/Diversion: Power, Intersections and Contradictions," in *Handbook of Workplace Diversity*, ed. Alison M. Konrad, Pushkala Prasad, and Judith K. Pringle, 299–322 (London: Sage, 2006).
2. Joan C. Williams, *Unbending Gender: Why Family and Work Conflict and What to Do About It* (New York: Oxford University Press, 2000).
3. Alan M. Webber, "Danger: Toxic Company," *Fast Company*, October, 1998.

6   The Old Boys' Network

1. Rosabeth Moss Kanter, *Men and Women of the Corporation*, rev. ed. (1977; reprinted with new Preface and Afterward, New York: Basic Books, 1993).

7 The Acceptable Band

1. Ann M. Morrison, Randall P. White, Ellen Van Velsor, and the Center for Creative Leadership, *Breaking the Glass Ceiling: Can Women Reach the Top of America's Largest Corporations?* (Reading, MA: Addison-Wesley Publishing Company, 1987).
2. Ibid., 13.
3. Ibid., 55.
4. Ibid., 57.
5. John T. Molloy, *The Woman's Dress for Success Book* (New York: Warner Books, 1977); and Betty Lehan Harragan, *Games Mother Never Taught You: Corporate Gamesmenship for Women* (New York: Rawson Associates, 1977).
6. Molloy, *Woman's Dress for Success.*
7. Nancy Levit and Robert R. M. Verchick, *Feminist Legal Theory: A Primer* (New York: New York University Press, 2006), 64.
8. Su Olsson, "Acknowledging the Female Archetype: Women Managers' Narratives of Gender," *Women in Management Review* 15, no. 5/6 (2000): 296–302; and Joan C. Williams, *Unbending Gender: Why Family and Work Conflict and What to Do About It* (New York: Oxford University Press, 2000).
9. Linda K. Stroh, Christine L. Langlands, and Patricia A. Simpson, "Shattering the Glass Ceiling in the New Millennium," in *The Psychology and Management of Workplace Diversity*, ed. Margaret S. Stockdale and Faye S. Crosby, 147–167 (Malden, MA: Blackwell Publishing, 2004); and Catalyst, "Women in Business: A Snapshot" (http://www.catalyst.org/files/facts/Snapshot%202004.pdf, 2004), accessed July 16, 2006.
10. Catalyst, "Women in Business: A Snapshot."

8 The Ideal Worker

1. Joan C. Williams, *Unbending Gender: Why Family and Work Conflict and What to Do About It* (New York: Oxford University Press, 2000).
2. Ibid., p. 39.
3. Williams, *Unbending Gender.*

9 Against the Law

1. Sara Evans, "Decade of Discovery: 'The Personal is Political,'" in *Perspectives on Modern America: Making Sense of the Twentieth Century*, ed. Harvard Sitkoff (New York: Oxford University Press, 2000).
2. Nancy Levit and Robert R. M. Verchick, *Feminist Legal Theory: A Primer* (New York: New York University Press, 2006), 59.

3. Evans, "Decade of Discovery."

4. Nicholas Lemann, "Taking Affirmative Action Apart," in *Affirmative Action: Social Justice or Reverse Discrimination*, ed. Francis J. Beckwith and Todd E. Jones, 34–55 (Amherst, NY: Prometheus, 1997); Lee Cokorinos, *The Assault on Diversity: An Organized Challenge to Racial and Gender Justice* (Lanham, MD: Rowman & Littlefield Publishers, 2003); and Stephan Thernstrom and Abigail M. Thernstrom, *America in Black and White: One Nation, Indivisible* (New York: Simon & Schuster, 1997).

5. Americans United for Affirmative Action, "Affirmative Action Timeline," http://www.auaa.org/timeline (site discontinued), accessed September 1, 1999.

6. Thernstrom and Thernstrom, *America in Black and White*; and Sara Wakefield and Christopher Uggen, "The Declining Significance of Race in Federal Civil Rights Law: The Social Structure of Employment Discrimination Claims," *Sociological Inquiry* 71, no. 1 (2004): 128–157.

7. Levit and Verchick, *Feminist Legal Theory*, 65.

8. Ibid., 73.

9. Ibid., 64.

10. Frederick R. Lynch, "The Diversity Machine: Moving Multiculturalism to the Workplace," in *Race in 21st Century America*, ed. Curtis Stokes, Theresa Melendez, and Genice Rhodes-Reed, 159–180 (Lansing, MI: Michigan State University Press, 2001).

11. Barbara J. Fick, "The Case for Maintaining and Encouraging the Use of Voluntary Affirmative Action in Private Sector Employment," *Notre Dame Journal of Law, Ethics & Public Policy* 11 (1997): 159–170; and Edward J. Erler, "The Future of Civil Rights: Affirmative Action Redivivus," *Notre Dame Journal of Law, Ethics & Public Policy* 11 (1997): 15–65.

12. Peter Ortiz, "Morgan Stanley Gender-Bias Case Could Shake Up the Street," *DiversityInc*, July 9, 2004.

13. Brenda Velez, "More Sex-Discrimination Charges for Morgan Stanley," *DiversityInc*, May 12, 2006.

14. Betsy Morris, "How Corporate America is Betraying Women," *Fortune*, January, 2005.

15. Bob Van Voris and Margaret Cronin Fisk, "Wal-Mart Probe Follows Decade of Sex Bias, Overtime Suits," *Bloomberg.com*, April 24, 2012.

16. Victoria Cavaliere, "Tennessee Women File Sex Discrimination Lawsuit Against Walmart," *New York Daily News*, October 2, 2012.

17. Joan C. Williams, Jessica Manvell, and Stephanie Bornstein, "'Opt Out' or Pushed Out? How the Press Covers Work/Family Conflicts," (publication of The Center for WorkLife Law, University of California Hastings College of Law, 2006), 45.

18. Brenda Velez, "'Crap' Comment About Women Indicative of Ad Industry?" *DiversityInc*, October 25, 2005.

19. Anne Fisher, "Why Aren't More CEOs Women?" *Fortune*, November 14, 2005.

10   The Toxic Workplace

1. Alan M. Webber, "Danger: Toxic Company," *Fast Company*, October, 1998.

11   Joy in Work

1. Herbert Applebaum, "Twentieth Century: Selected Philosophies and Perspectives of Work," in *The Concept of Work: Ancient, Medieval, and Modern*, ed. Herbert Applebaum (Albany, NY: State University of New York Press, 1992), 455–512.

12   Free Agency

1. Daniel H. Pink, *Free Agent Nation: How America's New Independent Workers are Transforming the Way We Live* (New York: Warner Books, 2001).
2. Joan C. Williams, *Unbending Gender: Why Family and Work Conflict and What to Do About It* (New York: Oxford University Press, 2000).

14   A Paradox of Diversity

1. Seth Lubove, "Damned if You Do, Damned if You Don't," *Forbes*, December 15, 1997; and Ron Stodghill II, "Getting Serious About Diversity Training," *Business Week*, November 15, 1996.
2. Rebekah S. Heppner, "A Paradox of Diversity: Billions Invested, but Women Still Leave," (PhD diss., University of South Florida, 2007).
3. William B. Johnston and Arnold E. Packer, "Workforce 2000: Work and Workers for the 21st Century," (Indianapolis, IN: Hudson Institute, commissioned by U.S. Department of Labor, 1987).
4. Taylor Cox Jr., "The Multicultural Organization," *The Academy of Management Executive* 5, no. 2 (1991): 34–47.
5. Ibid.
6. R. Roosevelt Thomas Jr., "From Affirmative Action to Affirming Diversity," *Harvard Business Review* 68, no. 2 (1990): 107.
7. Alison M. Konrad, "Special Issue Introduction: Defining the Domain of Workforce Diversity Scholarship," *Group & Organization Management* 28, no. 1 (2003): 4–7.
8. Robin J. Ely and David Thomas, "Cultural Diversity at Work: The Effects of Diversity Perspectives on Work Group Processes and Outcomes," *Administrative Science Quarterly* 46, no. 2 (2001): 229–273.

9. Gail Robinson and Kathleen Dechant, "Building a Business Case for Diversity," *The Academy of Management Executive* 11, no. 3 (1997): 21–31.

10. John M. Ivancevich and Jacqueline A. Gilbert, "Diversity Management: Time for a New Approach," *Public Personnel Management* 29, no. 1 (2000): 77.

Conclusion

1. Joan C. Williams, *Unbending Gender: Why Family and Work Conflict and What to Do About It* (New York: Oxford University Press, 2000), 245.

BIBLIOGRAPHY

Acker, Joan. "Hierarchies, Jobs, Bodies: A Theory of Gendered Organizations."
  Gender & Society 4, no. 2 (1990): 139–158.
Americans United for Affirmative Action. "Affirmative Action Timeline." http://
  www.auaa.org/timeline. Accessed September 1, 1999 (site discontinued).
Applebaum, Herbert. "Twentieth Century: Selected Philosophies and Perspectives
  of Work." In *The Concept of Work: Ancient, Medieval, and Modern*, edited by
  Herbert Applebaum, 455–512. Albany, NY: State University of New York
  Press, 1992.
Bird, Sharon. "Welcome to the Men's Club: Homosociality and the Maintenance
  of Hegemonic Masculinity." *Gender & Society* 10, no. 2 (1996): 120–132.
Catalyst. "Latest Catalyst Census Shows Women Still Not Scaling the Corporate
  Ladder in 2010; New Study Indicates Clue to Reversing Trend." Media
  announcement. www.catalyst.org, 2010.
———. "Women in Business: A Snapshot." Report. www.catalyst.org, 2004.
  Accessed July 16, 2006 (document no longer available on website).
Cavaliere, Victoria. "Tennessee Women File Sex Discrimination Lawsuit Against
  Walmart." *New York Daily News*, October 2, 2012.
Cokorinos, Lee. *The Assault on Diversity: An Organized Challenge to Racial and
  Gender Justice*. Lanham, MA: Rowman & Littlefield Publishers, 2003.
Cox Jr., Taylor. "The Multicultural Organization." *The Academy of Management
  Executive* 5, no. 2 (1991): 34–47.
Ely, Robin J., and David Thomas. "Cultural Diversity at Work: The Effects of
  Diversity Perspective on Work Group Processes and Outcomes." *Administrative
  Science Quarterly* 46, no. 2 (2001): 229–273.
Erler, Edward J. "The Future of Civil Rights: Affirmative Action Redivivus."
  Notre Dame Journal of Law, Ethics & Public Policy 11 (1997): 15–65.
Evans, Sara. "Decade of Discovery: 'The Personal is Political.'" In *Perspectives
  on Modern America: Making Sense of the Twentieth Century*," edited by Harvard
  Sitkoff, 162–176. New York: Oxford University Press, 2000.
Fick, Barbara J. "The Case for Maintaining and Encouraging the Use of Voluntary
  Affirmative Action in Private Sector Employment." *Notre Dame Journal of Law,
  Ethics & Public Policy* 1 (1997): 159–170.

Fisher, Anne. "Why Aren't More CEOs Women?" *Fortune*, November 15, 2005.

Harragan, Betty Lehan. *Games Mother Never Taught You: Corporate Gamesmenship for Women*. New York: Rawson Associates, 1977.

Hearn, Jeff, and David Collinson. "Men, Masculinities and Workplace Diversity/ Diversion: Power, Intersections and Contradictions." In *Handbook of Workplace Diversity*, edited by Alison M. Konrad, Pushkala Prasad, and Judith K. Pringer, 299–322. London: Sage, 2006.

Heppner, Rebekah S. "A Paradox of Diversity: Billions Invested but Women Still Leave." PhD diss., University of South Florida, 2007.

Ivancevich, John M., and Jacqueline A. Gilbert. "Diversity Management: Time for a New Approach." *Public Personnel Management* 29, no. 1 (2000): 75–92.

Johnston, William B., and Arnold E. Packer. "Workforce 2000: Work and Workers for the 21st Century." Indianapolis, IN: Hudson Institute, Commissioned by U.S. Department of Labor, 1987.

Kanter, Rosabeth Moss. *Men and Women of the Corporation*. 1977. Reprinted with new Preface and Afterward. New York: Basic Books, 1993.

Konrad, Alison M. "Special Issue Introduction: Defining the Domain of Workforce Diversity Scholarship." *Group & Organization Management* 28, no. 1 (2003): 4–7.

Lemann, Nicholas. "Taking Affirmative Action Apart." In *Affirmative Action: Social Justice or Reverse Discrimination*, edited by Francis J. Beckwith and Todd E. Jones, 34–55. Amherst, NY: Prometheus, 1997.

Levit, Nancy, and Robert R.M. Verchick. *Feminist Legal Theory: A Primer*. New York: New York University Press, 2006.

Lubove, Seth. "Damned if You Do, Damned if you Don't." *Forbes*, December 15, 1997.

Lynch, Frederick R. "The Diversity Machine: Moving Multiculturalism to the Workplace." In *Race in 21st Century America*, edited by Curtis Stokes, Theresa Melendez, and Genice Rhodes-Reed, 159–180. Lansing, MI: Michigan State University Press, 2001.

Molloy, John T. *The Woman's Dress for Success Book*. New York: Warner Books, 1977.

Morris, Betsy. "How Corporate America is Betraying Women." *Fortune*, January, 2005.

Morrison, Ann M., Randall P. White, Ellen Van Velsor, and the Center for Creative Leadership. *Breaking the Glass Ceiling: Can Women Reach the Top of America's Largest Corporations?* Reading, MA: Addison-Wesley Publishing Company, 1987.

Olsson, Su. "Acknowledging the Female Archetype: Women Managers' Narratives of Gender." *Women in Management Review* 15, no. 5/6 (2000): 296–302.

Ortiz, Peter. "Morgan Stanley Gender-Bias Case Could Shake Up the Street." *DiversityInc*, July 9, 2004.

Pink, Daniel H. *Free Agent Nation: How America's New Independent Workers are Transforming the Way We Live*. New York: Warner Books, 2001.

Robinson, Gail, and Kathleen Dechant. "Building a Business Case for Diversity." *The Academy of Management Executive* 11, no. 3 (1997): 21–31.

Stodghill II, Ron. "Getting Serious About Diversity Training." *Business Week*, November 15, 1996.

Stroh, Linda K., Christine L. Langlands, and Patricia A. Simpson. "Shattering the Glass Ceiling in the New Millennium." In *The Psychology and Management of Workplace Diversity*, edited by Margaret S. Stockdale and Faye S. Crosby, 147–167. Malden, MA: Blackwell Publishing, Ltd., 2004.

Thernstrom, Stephan, and Abigail M. Thernstrom. *America in Black and White: One Nation, Indivisible*. New York: Simon & Schuster, 1997.

Thomas Jr., R. Roosevelt. "From Affirmative Action to Affirming Diversity." *Harvard Business Review* 68, no. 2 (1990): 107.

Van Voris, Bob, and Margaret Cronin Fisk. "Wal-Mart Probe Follows Decade of Sex Bias, Overtime Suit." *Bloomberg.com*, April 24, 2012.

Velez, Brenda. "'Crap' Comment About women Indicative of Ad Industry?" *DiversityInc*, October 25, 2005.

———. "More Sex Discrimination Charges for Morgan Stanley." *DiversityInc*, May 12, 2006.

Wakefield, Sara, and Christopher Uggen, "The Declining Significance of Race in Federal Civil Rights Law: The Social Structure of Employment Discrimination Claims." *Sociological Inquiry* 71, no. 1 (2004): 128–157.

Webber, Alan M. "Danger: Toxic Company." *Fast Company*, October, 1998.

Whyte Jr., William H., *The Organization Man*. New York: Anchor Books, 1956.

Williams, Joan C. *Unbending Gender: Why Family and Work Conflict and What to Do About It*. New York: Oxford University Press, 2000.

Williams, Joan C., Jessica Manvell, and Stephanie Bronstein. "'Opt Out' or Pushed Out? How the Press Covers Work/Family Conflicts." Publication of The Center for WorkLife Law, University of California Hastings College of Law, 2006.

GENERAL INDEX

INDEX TO THE LOST
LEADERS' STORIES

Printed in the United States of America